First in the series of

An ABC of Eating Disorders

* * *

A is for Anorexia:
Anorexia Nervosa
Explained

* * *

Coming soon

B is for Bulimia

and

C is for Compulsive Eating

A is for Anorexia: Anorexia Nervosa Explained

Published by Process Press Ltd.

Text Copyright © 2015 Em Farrell

* * *

Offers

Find at www.abcofeatingdisorders.com

For everyone: a FREE Audio Book

A is for Anorexia: Anorexia Nervosa Explained (Route One)

* * *

For parents, family and friends

A FREE monthly support webinar with Em Farrell

* * *

For psychotherapists and counsellors a free chapter

'Body Products and Transitional Phenomena' from

Lost for Words: The Psychoanalysis of Anorexia and Bulimia

by Em Farrell

These are available at

www.abcofeatingdisorders.com

Table of Contents

A Guide to Reading This Book

This book has easy as well as relatively hard chapters to read. My own training, background, and experience of working as a psychotherapist means that a lot of what I am trying to do is make complicated theory accessible to everyone. If you are patient and perhaps know something of psychological theory I don't think you will find it too hard. But in case you do, I suggest three alternative routes through this book.

Route One: Easy. For parents, sufferers and helpers not wanting too much history and theory. If I were you I would read the 'Introduction', followed by 'Facts About Anorexia' 'Understanding Hunger', 'A Woman's Complicated Relationship with Her Own Body', 'How to Help', 'The Hard Labour of Recovery', 'How to Create Your Own Successful Care Package', and 'Conclusion and What Next'. If you become curious about understanding the mind of an anorectic go back and read the chapters you have missed.

Route Two: Medium. For sufferers who really want to understand: I recommend the whole book but the order you read it in might be different. I would start with the 'Introduction', then go to 'Hunger', followed by 'If Self-Starvation is the Answer What is the Question', then to 'Inside the Mind of An Anorectic', then 'The Hard Labour of Recovery', 'How to Construct Your Own Successful Care Package' and lastly the 'Conclusion' and 'What Next'. If you are still curious, go back and read the chapters that you have missed.

Route Three: Hard. For psychologically minded individuals: the whole book.

CHAPTER I

Introduction

This book is part of a series called *An ABC of Eating Disorders. A is for Anorexia, B is for Bulimia, and C is for Compulsive Eating.* I decided to write these books because I have worked in the field of eating disorders for almost 25 years and having written an academic book on the subject 19 years ago, I wanted to write books that are accessible and useful for everyone who has an interest in understanding eating disorders. I have been and still am fascinated and at times horrified by what women, and it is still largely women, do to themselves and their bodies in the hope of creating and living a good life or at least, attempting to do so. This book is for the sufferers of anorexia and their friends, families, loved ones and carers.

This may include social workers, hospital workers, counsellors or psychotherapists.

In order to escape the prison of anorexia the first step is to look around you very carefully, and to discover and get to know every inch of the space you are in. It is only then that you have a good chance of finding a way out. By the end of this book you will, if my plan works, be more empathic, towards yourself or the person you want to help and you will also be better informed about the mind and body of an anorectic and the hard process of recovery. You will realise that the process of recovery is like climbing Mount Everest. A once in a lifetime challenge. You will have to work hard physically, emotionally and psychically, and this applies to the sufferer as well as those around them. If you are anorectic you will, in fact be fighting for your life. It will require planning, commitment, energy and support from others. Being an anorectic takes a steely will, but if you can turn that will into the desire to recover, you can and will succeed.

My own interest in eating disorders started many, many years ago. When I was a teenager I had a school friend named Violet. What I remember was that she was beautiful, articulate and intelligent. She was a person of average weight, with quite a large dish shaped face and beautiful eyes. We were close friends and it was very disconcerting to see her losing weight over time and slowly disappearing in front of me. It was the late 1970s and anorexia wasn't that common or known about at the time. I didn't know what to make of what was happening. I knew she was unhappy and unwell but I didn't know how to help. I decided I would ask her to come on a holiday with my family.

My father rented a house in France. It was summer and quite hot. There was a swimming pool there as well. She seemed at ease at mealtimes and ate quite normally. Although she only ate the main course, but took a reasonable sized portion. This stopped me from feeling too anxious about her. But still she got thinner and thinner. I remember the strange quality of her skin that looked painfully drawn over her bones, particularly around her face. Her hands began to look too big for her body and were very red and seemed to flap at the end of her arms. Her hip bones stuck out in a sharp and starving manner. I remember her swimming after meals, on and on, as though she had some internal metronome she was keeping pace with. I felt left out, bewildered, sad and worried. It got to the point where she had to go home. I think she asked to go, but I can't quite remember. I think we all just knew she couldn't stay. I felt frightened and remember thinking I didn't want her to collapse on my watch. I also felt very powerless and distressed that I was not able to reach her emotionally, although I tried. It's a long time ago but her square face and her beautiful deep set eyes that seemed to be disappearing into their sockets made me want to understand, to know, what anorexia is about. So this book is for you, Violet.

You inspired me to want to understand what it means when a woman, any woman, chooses to take herself towards death by not feeding herself enough. Violet went into hospital and I saw her there a few times, but we lost touch soon after she came out. I think I caught sight of her once in the street. Though I wasn't sure, but I hope she made it. Although this book is primarily for women because that is the group that I have worked with and known, I am sure much of it will be relevant for male sufferers too. A good website for men who have anorexia is men get eating disorders too. The website address is: www.mengetedstoo.co.uk.

When I left university I did a variety of part-time jobs. One was being a massage therapist. I did some training in London and specialised in sports injury and pain work. What struck me very quickly was the very different attitude men and women have towards their bodies. Men tended to enjoy massages, and to take real pleasure in their bodies, but women usually did not. I became more and more aware of how uncomfortable women often feel inside their own skins. The sense was often of being presented with something ugly that I was expected to reject. Massage seemed to help decrease their level of physical self-hatred as they could experience my acceptance through touch, which then helped them accept themselves a little more. These were women who did not suffer from eating disorders.

So I decided to put these two experiences together, wanting to help women like Violet and those self-hating women I found on the massage table. I wanted to work with women's bodies directly to reduce their self-hatred and to work with their minds and help make sense of why they would misuse food, in whatever way they did. And with the experience of having trained as a counsellor with Nightline whilst I was a student I decided I would set up a centre for women with eating disorders. I did this in 1989 in London and began to see more and more people with eating problems. My idea was that touch could help establish a good emotional connection which could then prepare the ground for psychological change. This did indeed turn out to be the case. The model was a simple one. The standard format was 12 sessions, one a week, each an hour long, consisting of half an hour massage, followed by half an hour of talking. The model was based on a cognitive behavioural approach, CBT. And it worked. Over the years that I ran it, I saw close to 200 women, most of whom were symptom-free by the time they left. But there was a core group of women who did not get better and with whom I continued to work, as my own approach developed and changed as time went on.

I saw a number of women who had been anorectic and then became bulimic and I saw a few who were in a similar or worse state than Violet had been. As this book's focus is on anorexia, what I remember of the anorectics is that I saw how frightening they were; because there was always a risk that they might collapse. They rarely agreed to have a massage and if they did, it would often be through their clothes, and they would be sitting up. Because lying down and receiving touch would mean allowing me in, and also risking fainting on rising, or not managing to get up. I am, of course, at this point talking about extreme cases.

The thing I remember and that shocked me was seeing one severely anorectic woman on the massage table. In the British Museum there are two galleries on 'Egyptian death and afterlife: mummies'. And there in one of the cases, is an unwrapped, or as they used to say unrolled mummy. A woman. She is actually an old short woman, but she is just skin and bones and, no more. When I first saw Angela, with her body so similar to Violet's on the massage table, my mind went straight there and I felt sick, sad and worried that my touch might break her in two.

Some anorectics would not want to be touched at all. For those who did accept a very small amount, all their softness seemed to be gone, leaving nothing but a hard, vulnerable brittleness.

This book is aimed at understanding how and why anyone should in an age of plenty reduce themselves, by choice, to skin and bones. I really wanted to understand why people do this to themselves. I still do. How do they do it? What is the impact it has on themselves and those around them? How can you help them to do something different, or how can an anorectic choose to do something different herself ? I am going to use 'her' as 90% of anorectics are still women.

This is a big task but an interesting one. Every woman who develops anorexia does so for her own individual reasons. This book will guide you through some of the complicated reasons as to why this happens and hopefully help you feel more confident, as you try to navigate the anorectic world, either for yourself or a loved one. *A is for Anorexia: Anorexia Nervosa Explained* is the start. Next will be *B for Bulimia: Bulimia Nervosa Explained*, and finally *C for Compulsive Eating: Binge Eating and Obesity Explained*. Many anorectics have bulimic symptoms too, but in this book I am going to focus on making sense of the elements of anorexia that are not connected to bulimia.

One woman who wasn't helped by the 12 week programme was Claire. She came to see me when she was very anorectic, had one 2 minute massage, which was really just a back stroke through her clothes and could not tolerate it again. She stayed, as a patient of mine for over ten years; saw me through the pregnancy of my daughter and beyond. It is from her and our work together that I learnt a lot about what it is like to live in the land of anorexia and how incredibly hard it is to leave it and re-enter the world of the body and feelings. She has very kindly allowed me to write about the work we did together.

There are, of course, some overlaps between the books but right now, I want to tell you what I'm going to cover in this book. It is divided into eleven chapters. After this 'Introduction' is a chapter on 'The History of Anorexia'. In it I'll look at the striking similarity of the clinical picture of anorexia over time and how it has baffled and defeated clinicians for years. I'll look at some of the very different ways of understanding it, whether through the body or the mind. This will include some fairly recent psychoanalytic ways of making sense of the problem. Some of these ideas will then be explored in more depth, along with more current ways of thinking in the later chapter 'Inside the Mind of an Anorectic'.'

Before heading towards the individual cases that have taught me so much I'll give you the ice cold dope on anorexia in the chapter entitled 'Facts About Anorexia'. This chapter is full of facts and figures. What actually happens in the body and the mind of an anorectic and what the physical consequences are likely to be, depending on how long the person has been ill for, what age the illness started, how long it lasts for and its severity.

One of the defining characteristics of anorexia is the individual's curious and unusual relationship with hunger. I will look at this in the chapter on 'Understanding Hunger'. In it I shall look at the mechanisms of hunger and eating, physiologically and emotionally, and look at work of Ancel Keys and his research on what happens when you semi-starve people.

The women I gave massages to for sore shoulders or headaches all had issues with their bodies and they are not an unusual group. Many women have problems with how they look. Statistics in the West suggest that over 80% of women have some form of disturbed relationship to eating. So if you are a woman and you are reading this and you are not anorectic, you may find something you can identify with. You may find an anorectic part of you, even a small one. I want to find a way of identifying and making sense of this pernicious illness for anorectics themselves, their friends and their relations.

In my mind there is a continuum - a slippage from an everyday preoccupation with the body to becoming anorectic. The difficulty is that once the point has been reached when an individual can no longer turn back they end up in an anorectic land, which is different, profoundly different from the land of diets, and diets alternating with bingeing, that so many women know. This is part of what makes us so curious about anorexia. It seems so near and yet so far from most women's experience. How can people do it?

In order to find this out we need to understand how women feel in and about their bodies. Women's level of self-hatred about their bodies is mad. That is the only word for it. How can half the population hate themselves because of how they look? They want to be thinner, taller, different, usually other than they are. So understanding how this has come about, how a woman develops a sense of her own physicality and how she feels about her body may be an important precursor to why someone might or might not develop an eating disorder. So the chapter following 'Hunger' will be 'A Woman's Complicated Relationship with Her Own Body'. There is so much that has been written and spoken about bodies and hunger. My focus on these chapters is to gather all those threads together that I believe help to make sense of what happens for an anorectic.

The contextual cultural and social issues I am leaving for brighter minds than mine to deal with.

With Violet and with Angela on the massage table I found myself wondering that if starvation is the answer, then what is the question. This then became the title of the next chapter. My aim was to try and help discover what might trigger a person into starving themselves. Why it seems to be a solution at the time and the kind of thing it might be a solution to. In much of the literature on anorexia there is a split. A two way split. It is either seen as the fault of the parents, in particular, the mother, or as something that has happened because a young woman had dieted and that dieting has gone on and on. Often there is a question about fault. Whose fault is it? Why is my daughter anorectic? Why is my mother anorectic? Why is my lover anorectic? Why do I have anorexia? Is it the product of various factors in childhood and upbringing? Does the individual have a certain thinking style, a way of being, perhaps a genetic tendency towards anorexia? Questions abound. Understanding why someone becomes anorectic is a crucial part of their recovery and every woman who has anorexia needs to find her own individual answer. There is, of course, an urgency to discover why the person in front of you is so thin. They are sending us a message that needs to be decoded.

What matters is that no-one wants to create an environment where anorexia happens, neither the anorectic themselves, nor their loved ones, nor other women or men, but sadly it does happen and we do need to think about it. By the end of these chapters we'll begin to have some sense of why someone might become anorectic.

Then in chapter seven I shall move from facts to the inner worlds of some of the anorectics I have known. Part of what fascinates me about working as a psychotherapist is getting to know how people tick and what goes on in the secret corners of their minds. So I want to bring what being an anorectic is, in front of you. I shall introduce you to some of the courageous and some of the unreachable women I have worked with over the years.

Throughout the book you will meet women from the past, who were seen more through the eyes of men than through their own lens. Some of the women I have worked with will appear in these pages, as will some friends, family and interviewees. Over the years I have interviewed many women, some with current eating problems, and some with none at all, and some who are recovered eating disorder patients. Without these women this book would not have been possible. In the interests of their privacy I have on the whole disguised identities, and where I have not, either the person, or the information will hopefully be recognisable only to them. Claire will be the exception. Her own powerful presence and its impact on me will make itself felt through many chapters of this book.

On the whole getting inside the mind of an anorectic is difficult. That white door on the cover does not open easily, and when it does it is often a pretty scary place, full of unspoken and unknown demons. My first book was entitled Lost for Words: The Psychoanalysis of Anorexia and Bulimia. For all people who have eating disorders beginning to recognise that they have a body, how it feels and then putting these feelings into words is a Herculean task.

Chapter eight, 'How to Help' is designed to help you help. I will look at how you can help, whether it is yourself who needs help, or a daughter, a sister or a friend. It is hard to know what to do in the face of the profound denial of the woman in front of you.

Chapter nine is 'The Hard Labour of Recovery', where you

will find out how these courageous women fight for their own lives on a daily basis.

Sometimes of course, even our best efforts aren't enough. Sometimes we need someone outside of ourselves to help. In chapter ten 'How to Create Your Own Successful Care Package' I will be looking at outside sources of help for the anorectic herself. I will talk about the kind and mix of therapy that can help you move towards a better way of functioning. Seeking outside help and being well informed so you can make it work for you and your own situation is very important.

Finally in the 'Conclusion and What Next', I will try to pull everything together and then begin to take you into the world of the bulimic individual; to take you inside the bulimic ritual, which is so close and yet so far from the pure anorectic. The aim of this book is to open your eyes so that you can understand anorexia from the inside out and I hope to succeed. Do let me know what you think. Leave a comment at wherever you purchased the book or at www.abcoofeatingdisorders.com.

You can find out more about me in the 'About the Author' section right at the end, followed by 'Acknowledgements' and 'Other Books by Em Farrell'.

Thank you for buying and reading this book.

CHAPTER II

The History of Anorexia

The first recorded case of anorexia comes from the 11th Century. Anorexia nervosa, the full term for what is now usually referred to as anorexia is a very specific category of self-starvation, with its own particular set of physical, emotional

and psychological building blocks.

One early variant of anorexia was Holy Anorexia. Purity of spirit has often gone hand in hand with the mortification of the flesh. As Rudolph Bell, author of Holy Anorexia writes 'Death becomes a logical, sweet and total liberation from the flesh', and thereby an entrance to Heaven and immortality. Early examples of anorexia include Saint Hedwig of Andechs in the 13th century and Catherine of Siena who died of dehydration in the 14th century. So becoming anorectic was, for them, a way of becoming closer to God.

Anorexia was and still is a very mysterious and troubling problem. Richard Morton, working at the end of 17th

Century, saw two women who symptoms suggest they were anorectic. He wrote about them in his Pathisologica or a Treatise on Consumption. He described the symptoms as 'a nervous atrophy, a consumption of mental origin, without fever or dyspepsia, with the symptomology of food avoidance, amenorrhea, lack of appetite, constipation, extreme emaciation, and over activity' and says of one of them. 'I do not remember that I did ever in all my practice see one, that was conversant with the living so much wasted with the greatest degree of consumption (like a skeleton only clad with skin)'. She refused medication and died three months later.

He sounds shocked to me.

The term anorexia was first coined by two men working independently, on either side of the English Channel in the 1870s. Charles Lasègue in France and William Withey Gull, who was Queen Victoria's physician, in England, both saw people who did not eat and became thinner and thinner. They assumed these individuals had lost their appetite and so created the word anorexia, which means 'absence of appetite'. They were quite unaware at the time of how ravenously hungry these women were. Gull began by calling it anorexia hysteria. Hysteria meant connected to the womb. When he realised that men became anorectic too he changed the name to anorexia nervosa, which translates as the nervous absence of appetite.

Jean-Martin Charcot, a famous French neurologist and Professor of Anatomical Pathology who worked at the Salpêtrière Hospital in Paris in the late 19th century had a patient who wore a rose ribbon around her waist which she never untied. Her fear of fat, which she would become if she allowed herself to eat, was to be kept in check with the ribbon. He recognised what we now know so well that food itself is perceived differently when you are starving. He was also one of the first to recognise that an anorectic perceived her body in an unusual way. This is not quite as it seems, as we'll discover in the chapter on a woman's complicated relationship with her body. He also realised that anorectics were indeed hungry and he rechristened it 'anorexia gastrique', or gastric anorexia, which never really caught on.

Georges Gilles de la Tourette, a pupil of Charcot's, who gave his name to the syndrome he first described, put together a very important and up to that point, missing, piece of the anorectic puzzle. He realised how frightened anorectic patients were of their own hunger. It was not that they were not hungry. It was that they consciously denied that they were. So although the word anorexia remained Tourette reconceptualised the issue as being one of a fear of fat, really a fear of becoming fat. A fear of fat obviously means you have to be thin, as thin as possible, if you are going to avoid fat successfully.

Ludwig Binswanger, an existential psychoanalyst, wrote up 'The Case of Ellen West: An Anthropological-Clinical Study', in 1944. It is a poignant account of a young woman's attempt to deal with her trouble and troubling mind as she slips into the grip of an eating disorder, perhaps a mix of anorexia and bulimia. There are many of her own words in the case study in the form of poems and extracts from her diary. You will get used to hearing from her, directly and indirectly. Her dread of getting fatter was the central thought around which her world revolved. Binswanger tells us that on a walk with her husband she confesses 'that she is living her life only with a view to being able to remain thin, that she is subordinating every one of her actions to this end, and that this idea has gained a terrible power over her. '

Interestingly, these clinicians who worked with some of the first anorectics that we hear about thought that the disorder had a mental origin. They recommended that the first step in treatment should be the separation of the sufferer from the family, as there was a problem with the powerful influence that the parents, often the mother, had over the patient. Remember that these young women were being seen when they already had anorexia, which is enough to drive most parents close to the edge, and yet the very fact that this happens points to a consequence of anorexia. It leads to a greater involvement of parents, at a stage when most young women are in the process of emotionally and physically leaving home. Lasègue describes what can happen in a family: 'how the girl's condition and her refusal to eat gradually become the sole topic of conversation and preoccupation for the whole family'. So perhaps this difficulty of separating was hard to differentiate from being a consequence or a cause, or both, of anorexia.

Richard Morton, Gilles de la Tourette and Charcot believed that anorexia's main cause was psychological rather than physical. Lasègue and Gull started by looking at physical causes quite understandably before recognising that it had a mental not physical origin. It still is vital to check that there is no other cause for weight loss. If someone gets very thin, don't automatically assume that they have anorexia.

At the beginning of the 20th Century Maurice Simmonds, a pathologist at St. George's Hospital in Hamburg suggested that emaciation could be the result of pituitary destruction or deficiency. Indeed, the symptoms of Simmonds disease are similar, but sadly this meant for a period of time emotional and psychological reasons for anorexia were ignored. Once it was realized that Simmonds disease and anorexia were two different entities, with very similar symptoms, a return to thinking about the emotional reasons about why someone might become anorectic returned.

This move towards a different kind of understanding was helped by men like John Alfred Ryle who in 1936 discovered that psychosexual trauma could lead to amenorrhea (when menstruation stops). Most women these days, and most men, know that stress can indeed influence whether a period arrives or not. It may not appear at all or may be days or months late depending on what is going on. Ryle's work re-ignited interest in understanding the psychobiology of anorexia. This dance between the body and mind is particularly strong and complicated for anorectics. There is a weight below which a woman's body does not menstruate and research has shown that usually an anorectic's period will have stopped whilst her body, in terms of weight, is still capable of having them.

So how did people begin to try to understand and treat

anorexia nervosa?

Lasègue was so taken with the psychological factors that control appetite that he thought anorexia might be a way of avoiding pain, not physical, but psychological pain.

The body of the anorectic cannot be avoided and the treatment regimes devised in the last hundred years or so, are split in emphasis. One strand focuses first on the mind to cure the body.

The medical model focuses on wanting the body and mind of an anorectic to be understood and fixed. There is a hope of finding the answer. This group on the whole believe anorexia is outside the control of the anorectic sufferer themselves. They believe that, like schizophrenics, they are just wired differently and cannot help themselves. Some of their thoughts come from the research on semi-starvation. The main researcher in the field of hunger is Ancel Keys, who took 36 men in the 1940s and semi-starved them for 26 weeks before increasing their calories, or re-feeding them, as it is known. I'll look at his fascinating work in more detail in the chapter on hunger. His work showed that bodies, and minds to some extent, behave in a uniform way when they are starved. One of the things that happens is a narrowing of focus onto food itself, and recent research has suggested that anorectics have a particular way of thinking, where they focus on the detail of things, and this may predispose them to becoming anorectic.

The psychiatric approach wants to find a cause and then a cure. This is admirable, but so far the results haven't been very encouraging. The rates of recovery for anorexia and the failure to recover, which sometimes means death, have remained pretty consistent from the time that anorexia nervosa was first reported.

It is universally acknowledged that everyone in this world is different. This fact never ceases to astound me, and it is certainly accepted that everyone's heart and mind are different from another's, but medicine has always had to focus on the similarities, not the differences, which have led to the wonders of vaccinations, anti-biotics, heart bypasses and much, much more. Anorexia is of course a complex interaction between body and mind. Shinya Yamanaka, who won the Nobel Prize for Medicine in 2012 spoke in an interview about how the future lies in personalised medicine. It is being increasingly understood that each of us is physically and emotionally different and that means every anorectic has her own route to becoming anorectic, even though she may follow broadly similar paths to get there and every anorectic has to find her own individual path to recovery.

The unconscious

Sigmund Freud, the founder of psychoanalysis, many of his contemporaries and those who came after him such as Melanie Klein have very powerful and interesting ideas about what anorexia means. Unless you are versed in their ways of thinking their ideas have a tendency to sound pretty strange. It makes me quite hesitant to go towards them here, but I will tentatively do so. I am going to cherry pick the most edible and digestible ones. If you are a psychotherapist and would like to find out more, you can find it in my book *Lost for Words: The Psychoanalysis of Anorexia and Bulimia.*

The unconscious is mysterious and affects our actions in ways we don't understand. I like clarity, and one of Freud's early examples helped me understand its power, its simplicity and its mystery. A man is hypnotised and told that in response to a certain phrase he will put up his umbrella. The phrase is spoken and the umbrella raised. When the man is asked why he has put it up, he has no recollection of being hypnotised and gives a not very convincing but, for him, true answer. His unconscious was responding to something he was unaware of.

This is why I think some parents and doctors who work with eating disordered patients say that they are not choosing to have an eating disorder. In my view they are, but it comes from a place they don't know about and is about something they also don't know about. Our task is to uncover the mystery and help the unconscious become conscious.

I shall describe briefly how anorexia has been understood, before looking at the history of how anorectics have been treated. When I give workshops and lectures to psychotherapists and counsellors on how to work with eating disorders, I often put two words on the whiteboard. They are 'sex' and 'separation'. For me these are the areas that anorectics struggle with. So what do they mean?

There is an obvious way in which this is true. Anorectics often don't leave home, don't manage to have relationships, and with their absence of periods don't get pregnant. But psychoanalysts explore things in a more underground way and for anorexia the thought was that the thin body was a way of denying their own femininity and sexual appetite, because at some level they were very frightened of it. There are different strands to this, but saying 'no' to food was thought to be a way of saying 'no' to anything penetrating them. So they were saying no to sex, as well as to food. In some psychoanalysts' minds this was precisely because they were worried about how much they wanted, how powerful their urges were and how bad they felt about having them. Women are still not meant to be greedy.

Separation from the mother was thought to be essential. Charcot, in the late 19th century refused to take clinical responsibility in one case where the daughter, against his instructions, had not been removed from her mother's care. She was then taken into hospital, her mother sent away and she did recover. The complex issues around separation are very hard to unpick, and this is a very concrete example. When people have a difficulty unconsciously it is much more problematic, to explain, understand and work with. They cannot be aware of it. One way of starting to think about it, is that the child, and sometimes the mother have no real sense of being separate from each other. Go to chapters 'If Self-Starvation is the Answer, What is the Question? and 'Inside the Mind of an Anorectic' for more information on this complex topic.

The mind- body confusion of the anorectic

Hilde Bruch, a Professor in Psychiatry and a psychoanalyst, who worked in United States and who wrote about and worked with numerous patients with eating disorders, from the 1930s till her death in the 1980s, didn't find the defence against pregnancy fantasies that her fellow psychoanalysts did. She found that the women she worked with were fundamentally confused about their bodies. They couldn't work out what was going on inside them and couldn't begin to recognise the signals their bodies were sending them. This meant that they had no idea how to decode them. She found that her anorectic patients were at a loss. Once again whether this predated the anorexia or not is hard to know. In practice it remains a very useful bit of information. This is part of what someone with anorexia needs help with. Don't worry if you don't understand what this really means. It will, I hope, become increasingly clear.

It meant, for Hilde Bruch, that psychotherapists were not to leave the anorectic in silence in the consulting room. This would result in too much unmanageable anxiety, which the woman would not recognise as being anxiety, but which she would want to escape from. Instead you were to help her by naming what you saw her feeling and responding to, so that she could slowly begin to have some sense of what was going on inside of her.

There remains a real uncertainty about how to respond to anorexia. Only recently in the United Kingdom, a judge ruled that a young woman, close to collapse, who was surviving on half a bottle of vodka a day, was not to be force fed, because the risk of her killing herself was so great, yet paradoxically she was putting her life in danger anyway. There have been some really public tragedies, such as the death of Karen Carpenter and Lena Zavarone. Famous memoirs of anorectics have also been written, such as *Wasted: A Memoir of Anorexia and Bulimia* by Marya Hornbacher and the recent publication of a descendant of Virginia Wolf, Emma Wolf 's *An Apple a Day*.

Some psychiatrists in the United Kingdom have thought and worked long and hard on the subject. Peter Dally wrote a big tome in 1969 and split anorectics into three groups, the first being those who had obsessive components who often went on to overeat, those who were hysterical and who found it very painful to eat and the mixed group, of both types. Professor Arthur Crisp, author of *Anorexia Nervosa: Let Me Be and Anorexia Nervosa: The Wish to Change* saw anorexia as a response to the impossibility of puberty and growing-up. Both worked with, knew and cared for many, many anorectics. A different kind of knowledge comes from psychoanalysts who work with maybe only one, two or three anorectic patients, but work in depth, perhaps up to three, four or five times a week for many years. Harold Boris, in particular, has a clarity of expression of which I am very fond.

There are of course many current clinical experts in the field of eating disorders. In the United States Kathyn Zerbe and Philip Wilson come to mind. In the United Kingdom Janet Treasure, Director of the Eating Disorders Unit and Professor of Psychiatry at King's College, London has years of experience in the field. She writes informative and useful self help guides for families and sufferers, on her own and with others. The psychoanalytic tradition continues with books such as *The Anorectic Mind* by Marilyn Lawrence, and Susie Orbach's *Hunger Strike*. These are books I know and like and there are many more, but what matters is that the effort to understand, explain and attempt to help people liberate themselves from anorexia goes on.

The history of the responses to the problem do sometimes make me smile. Some of the early treatments, seem much more benign than the hospital ones I am about to describe. One that worked with an anorectic young man was the recommendation that he should go to the country, ride horses and drink a bottle of Madeira a day. He recovered.

Old fashioned hospital treatments

The basics are simple. If an anorectic is not to die they need to weigh more, and the aim of hospital treatment started off as simply being about re-feeding. The medical knowledge around starvation also supported re-feeding as a precursor to working with anorectics. It was thought they could not emotionally engage with therapy if they were at too low a weight.

There were and perhaps still are some quite scary treatments for anorexia. If someone is close to death and the decision is taken that they need to be fed then nutrition has to be given to them. Some people may be so weak, that they need to be fed through a tube. For some this comes as a relief, as they are not choosing to eat, and they do not have to put food in their mouths and chew. For others it is experienced as an awful assault. They could be being force fed against their wishes, to ensure they live.

I remember visiting Violet in a ward after she came out to stay with us. Her treatment was part of the deprivation regime, popular in the 1970s and 80s. All she had on the wall was a chart with her weight plotted on it. All her books, her radio, most of her clothes and the television had all been taken away.

At the start she wasn't even allowed pen or paper. The plan was simple. Everything of value was removed. She was given food to eat. She was not allowed to go to the bathroom for half an hour after she ate and when she did go, she was accompanied to ensure that she didn't try and vomit up the food.

If she ate and put on weight she was rewarded with something or someone. When I visited her she was allowed one book, a piece of paper, a pen and a visitor.

This worked. The aim was to have her put on weight. She did. There was a view, and as with so many things, I think it has some validity, that as starvation brings its own madness in its wake, if you deal with this then the person will be in a much better frame of mind to tackle their own distress. The difficulty is that anorexia has its own message to communicate, and unless this is understood this method of treatment will fail. It did with Violet. She came out, plump and within three months was back to her very thin self.

The trouble had not been sorted. Robert Bly, poet and translator of the classic Knut Hamsun book Hunger wrote in the introduction of the 1974 edition. 'There is a sense throughout the entire novel - that somehow his unconscious has chosen this suffering as a way for some part of him to get well.' Knut Hamsun condensed and fictionalised ten years of his life when he had been starving through poverty, into a period of some ten months. He was not anorectic, but this is such an important thought.

When faced with someone who is starving our impulse is to feed and focus on the body, but part of what we need to ask ourselves, is who is the person, this very small and thin person, and what are they trying to say and solve or sort out through this process of getting rid of themselves.

Good current provision

Nowadays thank goodness we now know that anorectics need help developing emotionally. It is as if a door has been shut which needs to be reopened. Eating has to be part of the picture of recovery, but only part. The crucial element is slowly helping the anorectic get to know themselves, to take their own lives, feelings and experiences seriously, and thus, begin to discover who they are.

There are now some very good eating disorder units out there. Some have in-patient re- feeding programmes along with a raft of different emotional therapies that are offered alongside. These might be art therapy, group therapy, individual therapy, (CBT or some other form), movement therapy, massage therapy, nutritional therapy or even equine assisted therapy.

Given how recovery is not only hard to achieve but to maintain as well, some services in America offer wrap around care, which follows the woman back out into the community and ensures that she has good support structures so that she keeps moving forward and if she gets stuck, someone is there who can spot the signs early and step in and help.

Remember

Charles Lasègue believed becoming anorectic was a way of avoiding pain. Hilde Bruch realised anorectics are in a muddle about how to recognise and make sense of the information they get from their bodies. These are the some of the key building of blocks about how we are going to make sense of this illness. Bear these things in mind when you are with an anorectic and also if you are anorectic yourself.

Chapter III

Facts About Anorexia

So now lets move from how anorexia began to appear on the medical scene and how psychiatrists and doctors tried to deal with it to some straight forward information about it.

I've put this chapter here, third in, because it is good to know the basics but also because of a curious turn of mind that anorectics have, which I will introduce to you here. If you have anorexia, more often than not you treat yourself as if your anorexia is an unchangeable fact. You often have little sense that what you are doing to yourself is problematic, until you stop doing it to yourself.

Anorexia is not about wanting to be thin in order to look like a super model. It might start off this way, but like the pot of gold at the end of the rainbow, becoming thin doesn't transform her life in the way she hopes it will. It is rather about trying to control a world that feels uncontrollable and that she does not feel part of. She attempts to restrict external and internal stimuli. Keep reading to begin to understand why someone needs to do this.

So what does this chapter cover?

It starts with the figures about anorexia nervosa, goes on to look at basic diagnosis, different kinds of anorexia, anorectic tactics to reduce food intake, food rules, how good it feels to say no, what a woman who has anorexia might actually eat and the mysterious role of liquid. Once someone has been anorectic for a while their body changes both externally and internally. All of the above, of course, have consequences, not only for the sufferer but also for those around or living with her. This leads to the tricky question of when you should intervene to save someone's life. I shall look at the Mental Health Act and how to spot when the time has come to take action on the sufferer's behalf if they are not willing or able to themselves.

Figures

The population of the United Kingdom is on the plus side of 64 million. NICE, the National Institute for Clinical Excellence believes 1.6 million people in the UK have an eating disorder and 10% of these have anorexia. These figures come from the National Health Service, so in reality they are probably higher, as they don't include private facilities or people who have never sought help.

In women between the ages of 18 and 25 in the United States anorexia results in 12 times more deaths than any other illness.

In the UK in recent years there has been a rise of 30% in incapacity benefit claimed on the basis of eating disorders.

The split between male and female anorectics has remained quite constant, despite the increase in men seeking ultra fit bodies. It may shift but currently remains at 90% of anorectics being female, with some 10% being male.

The scariest fact about anorexia is that between 10 and 20% of anorectics die. It has the highest mortality rate of any psychiatric illness, higher than schizophrenia or bi-polar disorder. The causes of death, although self-induced, vary somewhat, from dying from starvation, i.e., simply starving yourself to death, to suicide, to your body breaking down to such an extent, that recovery, even if you want it, is unlikely to be possible. This very nasty statistic needs to be borne in mind whether you have anorexia or are trying to help someone who does. The battle ahead is hard and may not be won. The longer you leave it the harder it is to recover.

Researchers who reviewed those who do recover found that 46% of anorectics go on to recover fully, 33% continue to improve and 20% remain chronically ill. These statistics are from the United Kingdom not worldwide, so figures might be different where you are.

I would add that these figures are looking at physical recovery; emotionally people often carry an anorectic mindset with them for life.

The basics of anorexia

Diagnostic criteria change somewhat, but this list is a simple one of some of the core behaviours and consequences that would lead someone to be diagnosed as anorectic. It is pretty much the same as it was in the 19th century.

The list starts with eating very little so that a great deal of weight is lost, not having periods, abusing laxatives, and/or diuretics, or exercise and, very importantly, denying that there is a problem. There is always a terror of fat and an extreme attachment to being thin. Often hyperactivity is part of the picture, as is an inability to sleep. If you are anorectic you will know this already and if you are not, but know someone who is, it will help orientate you to how bad things are or are not. The key emotional indicator of how unwell someone is, is how much they deny it. The intensity and depth of the denial of their body and its need for food and sleep is one way of working out how much help they need.

As William Withey Gull said in 1888, 'It seemed hardly possible that a body so wasted could undergo the exercise which seemed so agreeable'. And a turning point for Emma Wolf was when her boyfriend told her that her early morning running had to stop. She did stop but clearly found the request very hard to make any sense of at all.

I like how Hilde Bruch writes. She says of anorexia there is a 'pursuit of thinness in the struggle for an independent identity, delusional denial of thinness, preoccupation with food, hyperactivity and striving for perfection.'

Different kinds of anorexia

The literature and experts in the field tend to distinguish between two types of anorectics. There are restrictor anorectics and bulimic anorectics. The former group simply eat very little over very long periods of time, whereas bulimic anorectics eat very little for long periods of time and then occasionally binge. Their hunger has to be satisfied and they punish themselves for having succumbed to a need, either through taking laxatives, or self-induced vomiting or by throwing up. In this book the main focus is on anorectics who restrict their eating. As for those who have a bulimic element, this aspect will be more fully explored in B is for Bulimia.

Given the horrendous statistics about anorectics, I would like to use them to guide our thinking. Some people die as a result of being anorectic. Others remain chronically ill and live in a no-mans land, a kind of limbo, where they remain well enough not to collapse and land up in hospital but are never well enough to engage in life and eat in a way which allows them to have full access to their own feelings, energy and thoughts. They live a very limited, controlled, restricted life, but at least they are still alive. They are addicted to anorexia. It has run away with them. They have no hope or belief that they can shift, and this is why it is so important to understand what is going on inside them, so we can construct ways for them to come back to life, and out of the prison that anorexia so often becomes.

There is hope. Well over half of all women who get anorexia do recover or are in the process of getting better. It is easier when like Elizabeth, you are still consciously choosing not to eat, rather than feeling that you cannot. Elizabeth, who was never officially diagnosed with anorexia, began to eat very little, didn't menstruate until her early twenties, lost a great deal of weight, which she managed to conceal and deny, despite living at home. She knew it was a choice and one which she reversed because she was noticed, and felt, a little seen and attended to. She was brought back to life by a group of friends at school who challenged her about her anorexia and brought her food to eat, sweets which they bought with their own pocket money. Forty years on she still cries with relief and gratitude when she remembers this. When I asked her why she thought this worked, she was clear that she wasn't unduly attached to being anorectic and that some things in her school life were going well, like her work. But she added, 'I wonder if part of it was that I felt the game was up. I now had ten nosey children who would be on my case'.

This is obviously less hopeful for the anorectics who put their own lives at risk- people like Bernadette, who was beautiful and lived on tiger prawns and alcohol. She showed me photographs of herself as a three old, wearing a perfect dress, perfect shoes and with perfect hair; a perfect doll for her mother. She did not feel that she was seen at all. She looked extremely uncomfortable in her own skin. This is very similar to Karol, a patient of Hilde Bruch's who said, 'I never felt I was my own self. I was just a play thing'. Bernadette had a boyfriend who lived with her. Late in the evening she would periodically take overdoses and telephone me whilst doing so. Her boyfriend would often be in the adjoining room. She was in an agony of helplessness, despair and rejection. The combination of suicide attempts and her very low weight worried me greatly.

As she was at such a dangerously low weight, I said I would not be willing to work with her unless she stayed above a certain weight. She seemed so close to collapse and instinctively I knew she was slipping over the line where death becomes so tempting, and I was battling to try to keep her on the side of life. She agreed, and we began to do good work. She seemed to be able to be herself with me, to think that talking to me and allowing herself to feel her emotions might actually get her somewhere. I felt lighter, hopeful and also bewildered and doubtful. This seemed so unlike her. A thought that I didn't want entered my mind. Perhaps she'd lost weight. I thought she was looking thinner, but as she was much more engaged and seemed so different I wasn't sure. So I asked her, and she proudly told me she had fallen below the weight that we had agreed that she would keep to if I was to go on seeing her. She was triumphant at having deceived me. I felt conned and hurt. I reminded her of our agreement. She said she had no intention of putting on any weight, so we stopped working together. I felt foolish, as though I had failed to see something very obvious. You never know, but with her overt suicidal behaviour of overdosing and her slow suicidal behaviour of drinking a lot of alcohol and eating very little, her chances of surviving did not seem so high. Sadly, the lure of death seemed much more powerful for her than the lure of life.

People like Bernadette are rare in my experience, but they are likely to create an environment where preventing their death is a very difficult thing to do. I remember overhearing a psychiatrist talking on the phone about an anorectic in-patient, and saying 'Unless we can find a way to reach her, she is going to find a way to kill herself, either now, or after we discharge her'. The sooner you intervene the better, as someone is more likely to be able to reverse the process without having to go through the really tortuous work of reconnecting to their own body and then to the world.

Anorectic symptoms without denial

The behaviour, the not eating, is the same, but the individual's psychological relationship to it is different. They are much more likely to both notice and sometimes mind that they have lost weight. They are not in denial. This is the crucial difference and means something other than classical anorexia nervosa is going on. This means how you would treat them needs to be different. One of Hilde Bruch's patients didn't eat because she was convinced her hands might not place food in her mouth but would rather go to her neck and try to strangle her. So, for a small sub-group of these patients not eating can be a defence against psychosis or, indeed, part of a psychotic picture.

Another group which has anorexia without denial are the very old. But they know what they are doing and why in a conscious way. If an older person does this, it is often a hunger strike, usually born out of despair. The man or woman, (gender issues are less relevant here,) has simply turned their head to the wall and no longer wants to live. What is absent is the terror of becoming fat. For someone who is old, ill, lonely and in pain, finding a way to make life worthwhile can be very hard. So what they do have in common with the women and men who have anorexia is a loud 'No' to those around them. They feel unloved and unwanted and sometimes even are. Their 'no' to life is not a defence against a fear of living, but rather that they may have had enough of life, after many years of living it.

For some borderline individuals anorexia, and/ or bulimia and compulsive eating can be part of their clinical picture. Borderline individuals are chaotic; they try anything and everything to calm their incessant internal noise, which they are always trying to escape. Sadly, other self-destructive acts are usually part of the picture as well. They often play on the edge of life and death, by mis-using drink and drugs. They also often cut and burn themselves.

Lastly, there may, of course, be a physical reason why someone does not want to eat, or indeed why they may be losing weight. Do check this out and bear the pictures above in mind. How you need to proceed would be different.

Obsessive compulsive disorder and depression

Before looking at the nitty gritty of anorectic behaviour I want to briefly mention two ways of thinking and being that often go hand in hand with anorexia. The first is obsessive-compulsive disorder, a common companion to anorexia. This is obvious in terms of the young woman's relationship with food, such as not being able to eat before a certain time, or having to eat with certain cutlery and on certain plates in certain places. It can extend to hand washing and magical thinking: If I don't finish a particular task something awful is going to happen tomorrow. Or things have to be just so, pens in a line on my desk at just the right angle or I can't leave the room. I'm sure you know about this and can put many of your own examples in here. It, like anorexia itself, is a way of trying to solve things magically, to keep the person safe and to protect her from imagined dangers. Sadly, it tends to create problems of its own.

Depression is another common companion of eating disorders in general. In my view its most obvious trait is the presence of an internal enemy who simply kills hope and relishes hate, darkness and self loathing. When you feel you are wrong, drastically changing your body is one way to try to improve yourself and make yourself right.

Anorectic tactics

Given that anorectics are screaming to be helped with their bodies; whilst simultaneously denying their needs both to themselves and to the outside world, it is useful to think and know about the ways they use to prevent others and themselves from knowing about and really attending to what they are doing. This takes place along a continuum, both before and after the anorectic train may have run away with the individual. These tactics have remained consistent for the hundreds of years that anorexia has existed.

Anorectic tactics to reduce food intake

Water loading is one. This simply means drinking a lot of water, often before a meal, often as much as can be fitted in, to effectively reduce feelings of hunger and increase feelings of fullness. It is also used to deceive those who are weighing them about how much they weigh.

Eating very slowly is another. This is hard work. It was also a popular method of weight loss in Edwardian times, when people were encouraged to chew each mouthful 32 times. Anorectics slow down lots of aspects of eating. I remember one woman telling me how easy it was to make a Granny Smith apple last for two hours of a boring train journey. When you have very, very little of something it becomes extremely valuable, just like the research which shows that people who don't have very much money perceive coins to be larger than those who have enough. One part of the go slow regime is cutting the very small amount of food you have on the plate into smaller and smaller pieces, very slowly.

Another way is to get rid of the food you are given to eat. Ludwig Binswanger who wrote up the case of Ellen West tells about her deceiving her doctor by 'dropping food into her handbag', others slip it into their napkin, their pocket, give it to the dog or hide it under other food. Another alternative is simple withdrawal and avoidance. Anorectics have always apparently just eaten, or are not hungry at the moment. As they do and don't want their food habits to be noticed they will often avoid mealtimes as much as they possibly can, which is, of course, noticed but leaves open the possibility that they are eating at other times.

Having their own set of food rules

These are often as daft and eccentric as can be imagined. Their purpose is to shore up the ability to restrict eating substantially. Here are a few examples: 'I only eat a grapefruit and an apple on a Monday, a Wednesday and a Friday. 'I only eat roast beef and water' (from the 19th century). 'I have to cut everything I eat into 6 pieces.' 'I cannot eat before 8.17 pm.' 'I can only eat in a clockwise direction.' 'I can't eat using that knife and fork.' ' I cannot eat any food on my plate if it touches any other food. "I only eat green food.' I am sure you can add your own rules and regulations to this list. Miss R, a patient of Henri Rey's, got to the point where she would not eat food at all, but would willingly accept being fed through a naso-gastric tube.

How good it feels to say no to food

If you are a friend or a family member of someone with anorexia this is an important one. Don't underestimate it. It is delicious, delightful and powerful to know that unlike people around, you are able to say 'No'. You can watch people say,

'Oh, I really shouldn't eat that' and feel superior, in control, and strong rather than weak-willed. You can also sit with your family and eat very little. It is very hard to sit there but there is also a kind of satisfaction in it. As Elizabeth said, 'I was winning a race which interested my fellows. There would be much less sense of triumph if half the people around us were not also fairly obsessed about weight'.

It is not just about power and control; hunger itself feels good, really good. Kathy, a woman I saw, who had been anorectic and then moved on to being bulimic, was very angry that people didn't know and didn't write about how much fun it was. That it gave her a high which she really missed once she gained weight and ate more normally. As Emma Wolf says of her hunger, it was a 'clean, empty high'... 'Forget cocaine, forget ecstasy, this is the best high I have ever known'. This grip that anorexia can have on the body, as well as the mind is going to need something or someone very persuasive and persistent to shift it.

What anorectics actually eat

A few examples will suffice. One of Hilde Bruch's patients, Beth, who studied nutrition, decided that three chicken livers a day was perfect. Eric, when asked if he ate his breakfast, replied

'Yes, I had my cheerio'. You will often find that a number of foods are allowed, sometimes in very specific amounts and sometimes freely. One woman I knew ate only sweets in the daytime and in the evening allowed herself little bits of chicken, some dry cereal and cucumber. Sally lived on toast and chocolate and Bernadette, who we have already met tried to survive on tiger prawns and white wine. Poor Dora, who died, tried and failed to live on sticks of celery and chewing gum.

The mysterious role of liquid

For anorectics food is the problem and food is not drink. So, for some, liquids have a special place. For a few, it is alcohol, like doll-like Bernadette who would consume a bottle of wine at night without thinking of the calories, or Natalie who used drinking alcohol as a step to allowing herself to widen her food choices or, indeed, Emma Wolf who could go out for a drink without much comment or thought. It is as though for many anorectics the calories in what they drink don't seem to count.

How an anorectic attempts to prevent detection

Few anorectics want their bodies to be seen. They are often cold, so wearing big, loose clothes is sometimes a clue. For this will both keep the individual warm and make it hard for others to know exactly what size the person is.

Often part of the recovery regime is being weighed. If this is by a doctor or nurse, without much knowledge of anorexia, then the battle is on. As Elizabeth, one of the most honest and ethically driven women I know, said when she was asked what she weighed, 'I just lied'. The woman who is being weighed will ensure that she weighs what she thinks she needs to, to prevent detection. This may not be how much she actually weighs, but there are things that can help. Once again, drinking lots of water before the moment of truth puts weight on, as does putting stones in your underwear. I remember being really shocked when Violet told me she did this. She also put weights in her coat pockets and shoes. Every woman who has ever dieted knows how to do this in reverse.

The scariest and hardest weapon in the anorectic arsenal is that of denial in the face of this anorectic behaviour and its consequences.

Visible physical consequences

The most obvious one is weight loss. Hands and fingers can become very red, and if obsessive behaviour is part of the picture, very dry, as a result of endless hand washing. The symptoms listed below are when things get very bad.

Hair gets thinner on the head and sometimes falls out. At

the same time soft, downy hair called lanugo, may appear on the arms and legs.

Lynn Crilly, a mother of an anorectic daughter and author of *Hope with Eating Disorders*, says that the eyes are the things that give the major clue, in that they become sunken, hollow and haunted.

When a body gets very thin it is very hard to keep warm, and so if you have anorexia you will feel very cold, dread the winter and need to keep your room or home very warm in order to manage.

Peripheral oedema occurs in some 20% of anorectic patients. This is where peripheries swell, whether fingers or, more commonly, legs. It has a number of possible causes and can occur both in the active anorectic phase and during the process of regaining weight.

As circulation becomes difficult the hands can become blue.

Internal physical consequences

When speaking about the different levels of anorexia, part of the difficulty arises when the individual gets too fond of starvation, which brings certain consequences in its wake. In the chapter on hunger we will look at Ancel Key's work which so influenced how we think about and treat those who are starving.

The impact of not having periods depends on a number of things. One is on whether they start at all. A few young girls become anorectic pre-puberty, as do boys and this can cause horrendous damage, as the body is starved at a time when it needs to be growing. I remember going to a talk and seeing photographs of a young boy's feet, which were on their way to getting gangrene as his circulation had become compromised due to starvation. If a young girl's body is not given adequate nutrition, she does not start to menstruate, which can lead to fertility problems in later life, although often the body can recover well.

If she does have periods, and they then stop due to her anorexia she is at an increased risk of developing osteoporosis. This is the brittle bone syndrome of post menopausal women. If a woman starves herself for a long time and doesn't have her periods, one of the defining characteristics of being anorectic, then her bone density is likely to be affected. This means her bones become more fragile, and even a knock or a fall can lead to broken bones. I remember hearing of one anorectic woman who after her stay in a half-way house left on crutches due to multiple fractures. I recently read a heartbreaking blog written by a woman determined to give up her anorexia, but who had a couple of crumbled vertebrae, which meant potential paralysis. Her desire for recovery came too late to escape some very nasty and long-term physical consequences.

It hurts to be so thin; not only are you going to be very cold, but sitting in the bath will hurt your tail bone and sitting on certain chairs will be painful. Sleeping can be hard, because you fear you may die and you don't have the energy to turn over.

Your blood pressure may get so low that you are in danger of collapsing.

The stomach can take longer to process food and severe constipation can occur.

Your heart may start behaving erratically and you can risk cardiac arrthymia, which can lead to a heart attack.

Your organs may begin to fail.

The impact on those who live with or work with anorectics

When I gave my first talk about eating disorders entitled 'Bulimics and their Bodies', the man who asked me to give the talk very kindly asked me to spend the evening with him and his family. He told me he'd put on two stone in weight since he started working with anorectic patients. He found himself frequently eating after the therapy sessions he offered. It is as though the hunger was passed from them to him without words.

Another reason a person close to an anorectic may gain weight is the vicarious thrill that an anorectic can get from feeding another. Hilde Bruch talks of Dora, one of her anorectic patients, who became obsessed that her brother was starving and always carried cake and candy for him. Not surprisingly, he ended up becoming quite obese.

Parents and siblings

The terror that having an anorectic in the family creates is difficult to imagine unless you have been there. The focus shrinks to watching and waiting to see if she is going to eat, engage, be ok or not. Is she going to make it through the day? And what kind of a day will it be? Is she going to talk to you? Is she going to sit and eat or not eat with you? Are you or her going to lose your cool? Who is going to end up crying? Parents' anxiety and distress will obviously be very high and on-going and they might need help themselves to manage the torture of having an anorectic child. Siblings also need support as they are likely to receive much less attention than their anorectic sister. They understandably will have very strong feelings towards her, both of love and concern, and frustration and rage that she is causing such havoc in the family and is so unhappy.

Staff in eating disorder units

The drop-out rate of staff in eating disorder units is very high. As Janet Treasure says 'staff burnout, sickness or difficulties with recruitment and staff continuity frequently occur'. She goes on to say that staff often want to overprotect the sufferer of anorexia, a very common response when someone is so extremely physically fragile in front of you.

Do I intervene to save someone's life?

There is a major philosophical debate about whether to intervene on behalf of someone who wants to take their own life. Psychotherapists vary in their beliefs. Some think having the right to life, also means having a right to end it.

There was a time when I believed this. Perhaps in some cases I still do, but with 99% of anorectics I don't. I want to help them find and fight with the tiny healthy, light seeking part of them which is there somewhere. This, in my view, is why in the United Kingdom; the Mental Health Act exists.

Some of the bad signs are unsurprisingly to do with weight. So I just want to explain what BMI means, as you'll see it mentioned a few times in what comes next. BMI stands for Body Mass Index, and is your weight in kilograms divided by your height in metres squared.

Bad signs

If she is so cold that she needs the heating on all the time. If her hands and feet look blue

If she gets dizzy and feels faint when she stands up

If she has puffiness and swelling around her eyes and has swollen ankles in the afternoon

If she has difficulty raising her arms

If her BMI is less than 15 she should have regular ECGs. If she has tachycardia, which means her heart is beating too fast, she should be hospitalised.

The Mental Health Act

The Mental Health Act in the United Kingdom is at core intended to protect those who put their own or others lives in danger.

If someone has a BMI of less than 13.5 they are likely to be in severe danger.

Spotting when her life is at risk

If she has a seizure

If her heart rate is very fast If she is sleepy or twitchy

Or has pins and needles in her toes

If her hands twist involuntarily into spasms

Janet Treasure suggests a couple of practical tasks to gauge how unwell she is and to see if she needs to be hospitalised, either voluntarily, or sectioned under the Mental Health Act.

The first is asking her to get up from lying down without using her arms and the second is asking her to rise from a squat without using her arms.

You need to take action if she cannot do either of these things.

Remember

Knowledge is power. However painful these things are: it is good to know.

CHAPTER IV

Understanding Hunger

Beginnings

We all start off hungry. We are programmed so that when we are born. A baby placed on a mother's stomach will crawl, yes, crawl up to the breast to feed, when only a few moments old. So right from the start there is, in fact, little else that is driving us. The search for nourishment is what ensures our survival. Yet even now we are different from each other. Alessandra Piontelli studied twins in the womb. She scanned them regularly and watched how they behaved. She wanted to see if the behaviour inside the womb continued once the babies made it into the outside world. It did. I remember reading of one twin who was often observed licking the umbilical cord. Then as a baby too, she continued to love licking and eating.

So hunger gnaws but differently from one person to another. Remember this. If hunger was an unimportant issue in an anorectic's life it is unlikely that they would turn against it with such force. My hunch is that for many, they are terrified of their hunger, their desire and their appetite. Sigmund Freud, the founder of psychoanalysis, was very aware of this and in a now in many ways dated but delightful quote says of babies who are keen on sucking:

'If that significance persists, these same children when they are grown up will become epicures in kissing, will be inclined to perverse kissing, or, if males, will have a powerful motive for drinking and smoking. If, however, repression ensues, they will feel disgust at food and will produce hysterical vomiting... Many of my women patients who suffer from disturbances of eating, *globus hystericus*, constriction of the throat and vomiting, have indulged energetically in sucking during their childhood'.

Anorexia certainly qualifies as eating disturbance. Hunger starts off as being a terrifying demand for all of us. That small newborn making its way to the breast has to then negotiate a lot when it arrives. It has to find the nipple, latch on successfully and suck. If this all goes according to plan then colostrum, the nutrient rich substance in the mother's breast flows pleasurably into the baby's mouth and body.

So far, so good. But rather like a friend of mine saying after her first day of school, that she had been to school now and wasn't that it? She didn't realise that she had to go again and again. This process of getting hungry and being fed goes on and on and on and is rarely simple. Hunger and the body are of course inseparable and for a baby, hunger gnaws. It does so in a way that feels scary and intolerable. It hurts, sometimes a lot. That is why babies cry for food. Because they have no way of making sense of what they are experiencing, no words, no conceptual framework, in fact, no idea of what is happening. It terrifies them.

Psychoanalytic ideas suggest that it feels as though they are under attack. Something is coming at them from outside which is causing them pain. The knife has gone in and they cannot work out what direction it came from. They do know they don't like it and their only response is to scream. On a good day someone who can feed them, their mother, father, or carer will appear and as the milk streams out of the nipple, false or real, the baby's pain will begin to subside.

When things go according to plan

Becoming a person is hard work and even when everything goes according to plan it is still pretty difficult. Hunger hurts and a baby is totally dependent on others. In the early days good new mothers or fathers attune themselves, with automatic hypersensitivity to the needs of their new baby. They are acutely aware that this tiny person's life lies in their hands. They respond quickly when a baby cries and try to discover what the matter is.

Melanie Klein, a psychoanalyst who was very interested in early development, thought the baby had an idea of a mother or carer who gave and provided food and love and touch and one who didn't. She felt the baby metaphorically had in her mind a good provider of food, symbolised by Klein by the breast, and a bad one. The good one was the one that came when needed and helped the pain of the hunger be replaced by the satisfaction of fullness, often accompanied by a feeling of sleepiness, pink cheeks and deep relaxation. On the other hand Klein thought the baby began to experience the person who didn't come straight away when needed, or was not able to make things better instantly as the person who was causing them pain. It became their fault. Given that a baby doesn't have words I am taking some dramatic licence here. So in the baby's mind Klein thought there lived two representations of the main carer, a goody and a baddy and for the baby a major development move is when the baby realises the person they love and who cares for them is also the person who abandons and hurts them. This leads to knowledge of powerful feelings of love and hate and the beginning of guilt and a desire to repair damage when angry feelings get out of control. So this is what should happen if all goes according to plan.

For psychoanalysts a baby feeding is the early concrete prototype of how we begin to take things in, digest them and make good use of them.

When things don't go according to plan

Implicit in the successful scenario is that the person who cares for the baby learns to help the baby distinguish between different kinds of discomfort. So that hunger can be differentiated from being too cold or too hot; or having indigestion or needing to do a pee or a poo, or having teeth coming through, or any other complicated sensations that a baby's body can produce.

As it is quite a complicated process there are many stages and ways in which things can go wrong in the successful recognition and response to hunger. Here are a few:

When a baby gets too hungry, a universal response to pain is rage and once the baby is consumed with anger it may not be able to eat when the bottle or breast is presented to him or her. So the baby may indeed reject the very thing it is so wanting and needing. Research shows that a baby cannot digest food unless he or she is relaxed. A tense child cannot digest, so a carer's first task is to soothe and calm a baby, so that it is in a physically calm enough state to eat.

The baby provides the hunger. Someone else has to satisfy it. Here too things can go wrong. I'm reminded of the couple who accidently killed their baby. Leroy Elders was only 3 months old when he died after being poisoned by taking in too much salt. His parents had liquidised adult food for him. They certainly did not mean to kill him, but they did. If a mother wants to breast feed her milk may not come in or her baby may be tongue tied and unable to get as much nourishment as he or she wants and needs. The mother may develop sore breasts or mastitis and decide the pain of breast feeding isn't worth the benefits. Some others may decide not to breast feed at all. They may link breasts with sexuality and not feeding. Or a woman might not want to because she doesn't want her breast shape to change. Some women choose not to breast feed and some are not able to.

Psychologically, regardless of whether a woman breast feeds

or not, if she is happy with her decision things are likely to go well. For a mother who really wants to breast feed and is struggling to do so, things can go wrong. If a mother is anxious, which produces tension in the body, her milk is less likely to come in. If a baby is placed on the lap of a unconsciously tense mother she or he is likely to tense up themselves, thereby making feeding difficult for them both. If a carer is bottle feeding his or her baby and is very anxious and worried, this may also impact negatively on the baby.

Some babies simply turn their heads to the wall and fail to thrive, when food alone is provided and not the body and heart of another. There will be more about the importance of the body in the next chapter.

A couple of examples will suffice to show the complexity of this area.

The first is a mother whose newborn was not feeding and was very distressed. One look at the mother and you could see she was terrified. In her mind breasts were only related to sex. She felt very confused. No one had helped her work out or indeed told her that breast feeding can be pleasurable. It gives the mother and the baby a release of oxytocin, the somewhat incorrectly named bonding hormone. It helps the mother relax. It is sensual and that is ok. A friend then came and sat with her and told her about how much she enjoyed breast feeding her child. The woman looked less worried and like magic the baby began to feed.

The second example is of a woman who had an old fashioned nurse to help her through the first six weeks of her baby's life. The mother wanted to breast feed and did so, but not for long. The nurse insisted on weighing the baby after each feed to see how much milk it had swallowed. Physiologically, I don't even know that it works this way, but this nurse could not bear not to know how much milk the baby was getting.

We know a lot more about breast milk than we did in the 1950s. We know it has different levels of water, nutrients, depending on the time of day, the temperature and crucially, that the body of a mother knows how much milk to produce. It responds superbly and accurately to the demands of the baby. It is a good system that works pretty well, although, this too can be fraught with difficulties. But not surprisingly, this poor mother was persecuted by the nurse and gave up breast feeding in favour of bottle feeding. Then the nurse could control and see how much milk the baby was getting.

Post babyhood hunger and feeding

Donald Winnicott, a paediatrician and psychoanalyst came up with the term a 'good-enough mother'. This is the best kind of mother anyone can be and involves allowing the baby the gradual experience of disillusionment. This happens anyway. Perhaps in the first few hours, or the first few days, or even during the first few months carers leap to the baby when it cries, but as time goes on, if the parent is not too anxious about the baby's survival, they will begin to trust that he or she will survive a minute or two or longer until they are fed. The timing has to be just right, so that the baby can tolerate the wait and is not pushed into an anxious and angry state that he or she might have difficulty recovering from.

This capacity to wait and tolerate frustration is a vital part of learning how to be human and parents or carers who respond to all cues with feeding create confused and often overweight or compulsive eating children. I shall look at this in more depth in *C is for Compulsive Eating*.

Feeding your child workshops

Feeding and being fed is a complicated business. I used to run, sadly, with not a great deal of success, may I add, workshops on feeding your child. The aim was to show parents how complicated it is and how you cannot separate feeding children from the person who does the feeding, their own story, their own relationship with their body, and the societal and cultural meanings we attach to food.

We all live in an environment, where calorie rich, nutritionally poor food is too available on one hand and, on the other, is the fattist and body-hating environment.

Both of these things interfere with our sensible response to hunger. So when a couple comes together to have a child they will have to make decisions about how they are going to feed him or her. They will have their own familial rules about eating which normally come from their own childhood. So some negotiation between partners may be required straightaway. Do you have set meal times? If so, when are they? Do you have to finish everything on your plate? Can children eat between meals? Maybe you never sat down to eat and just helped yourself from the fridge when you wanted food. Maybe you don't think children should eat sugar or fat, or perhaps there wasn't a table to eat at, and you always ate in front of the television.

This is before any issues of gender and weight come into the picture directly. Women who are bringing up children are often very worried about how and how much to feed their children. As Susie Orbach discovered, so sadly but brilliantly when researching *Fat is a Feminist Issue* women fed their baby boys for a longer time than their baby girls. This classic was written in 1973. Most women are preoccupied about what and how much they are going to feed their children, and the meaning they give to food impacts their children in different ways.

Food and eating can become a battleground at any age, but the majority of anorectic cases start in adolescence.

Hunger and adolescence for girls

Adolescence is a time of movement from child to adult, and from home out into the world. In the Western world it is also a time of immense intellectual pressure, with exams and an uncertain future ahead of you. Hunger is something that is often played with as a way to help manage anxiety, either by over- or under-eating, or by becoming vegetarian. Having different food habits than your parents is another way of trying to separate from them. For a parent, feeding a child has meaning. It takes work, money and labour to produce food day in and day out for a family. It represents love and when children reject food it hurts. It can feel like a personal rejection and sometimes it is meant to be.

Ideally

The ideal is simple: we know when we are hungry, we respond to it by thinking about what we would like to eat and we stop when we have had enough. Yet, this is rarely straightforward as, Henry Jaglom, director and writer of *Eating: A very serious comedy about women and food*, said, "Each woman I've known has been, in some significant way, deeply and profoundly and undeniably involved with food."

Satiety

Metabolically, we are all programmed differently; from how hungry we are, to how quickly we feel full. People are designed to be of different sizes. Our bodies have a set point that they naturally gravitate towards if eating was only about responding to physical hunger cues and satisfying them. This is known as 'set point theory' and research suggests it takes some three years at a new weight for our bodies to adapt to it. Given that the average length of time that someone is anorectic is seven years, they have with extraordinary willpower and determination ignored and denied their body for a good three years before it became somewhat easier to do.

Hunger and society

So much has been written about how women need to shrink themselves to fit in with a patriarchy where they are not meant to take up too much space, emotionally, intellectually and physically. An awful lot of women who aren't necessarily anorectic have trouble with their appetite. Emma Wolf wrote a column about her anorexia in *The Times* and says she didn't realise 'how bad women felt about their appetites, about being hungry and needing food and the simple act of feeding themselves'. One woman used to tell me that if you put her in a sweet shop she would want to eat everything.

Are you hungry when you are starving yourself ?

In the early days of anorectic research the assumption was that people who chose not to eat weren't hungry. Most women and increasing numbers of men know that this is not the case. If you have dieted you will remember the way your internal focus narrows - how the experience of hunger can be relished and befriended. It can make you feel superior. It leads to the kind of thoughts like 'I am managing to resist temptation when others fall for it'. So many women, not those who are anorectic, but those of us who have ever dieted, talk of a switch, which when flicked and causes us to move from eating what we normally eat to eating much less. In doing so we become increasingly aware of our bodies and our hunger and are choosing with quiet control how to ignore what our body needs and wants. This is where women who diet live and the high of hunger can be hard to give up.

Anorectics are hunger experts

The most famous study on hunger is that undertaken by Ancel Keys and his colleagues in 1944 at the University of Minnesota. In it he took 36 conscientious objectors out of some 200 who volunteered in a response to an advertisement: 'Will You Starve So That They Be Better Fed?'. The participants were chosen for their solid emotional and physical constitutions. At the time little was known about either starvation or about how you started to feed people safely after they had suffered starvation for a period of time. It was an important issue, as by the close of the Second World War, many people were very short of food, and some countries had been suffering close to famine conditions. A way to re-feed them safely needed to be found. It was known that if you just let starving people eat what they wanted it could lead to death. We'll look at how to safely re-introduce more food in a later chapter, but for now I want to describe the study and look at what happened to these men's bodies and minds as a result of their long period of starvation.

Almost all of the facts below come from a very readable book by Todd Tucker called *The Great Starvation Experiment: Ancel Keys and the Men Who Starved for Science* and an article by Leah M.Kalm and Richard Semba, published in 2005 in *The Journal of Nutrition*.

Keys began by working out the men's usual calorific expenditure, and had them exercise regularly. They had to walk an additional 22 miles a week, as well as the two or three miles a day to and from their lodgings. He then reduced their food for some 24 weeks. Interestingly, he decided how much weight each man was due to lose and then, if they didn't, he reduced their calories even further. People's response to calories does vary, even when you keep the output apparently constant. Keys didn't like this and he even refused to include one man's data in the study, because he had not lost enough weight, despite having his calories reduced and reduced. He was one of the most muscular and fittest of all the men on entry. By the end of the starvation phase the men who remained had bodies that were reminiscent of concentration camp survivors. The difference was the smiling faces they put on for the press.

Keys research is fascinating and has guided a lot of thinking about anorexia and what happens to someone who chooses to cut back on their food dramatically. There are, of course, a few crucial differences that need to be born in mind. These men chose to take part in the experiment, and all their food and routines were arranged for them. They were not starving themselves as a response to distress with how they looked or felt but were doing it to help the war effort and they were men not women.

What Keys and his team discovered in the semi-starvation phase was that the men became obsessed about food. All became fascinated with food itself and found waiting for their meals close to intolerable. This was a change for many of them who had previously not really noticed food in their lives. They also took longer and longer to eat their small portions, and some would hide food and take it back to their dormitories to eat it in secret later. Robert Willoughby puts it: '... eating became a ritual ... Some people diluted their food with water to make it seem like more. Others would put each little bite and hold it in their mouth a long time to savor it. So eating took a long time.' Sam Legg got very frustrated if there was any interruption when he was being given his food in the canteen.

He could not bear to wait. He ate away from the others and mashed up all his food together into a gloop and then finished it off by licking the plate. Many of the men, including Sam, began to collect cook books. Indeed, Carlyle Frederick had close to a hundred books by the time the study was over.

Their sex drive and ability to concentrate both reduced as they lost weight. All of them became very interested in their bodily functions, and focused more on their bodies as they changed.

The things listed above were common to them all, but we are all different and the men also responded in their own individual ways.

Gum and black coffee was allowed in unlimited amounts, and two of the men regularly consumed 40 packets of chewing gum a day.

Some didn't make it to the end of the experiment. Franklin Watkins, very near the start of the experiment, began having dreams of cannibalism. He felt so bad that he began to cheat and eat. His guilt then persecuted him and he promised to stop cheating. He found he couldn't and then threatened to kill himself or Keys. He was taken to a local mental asylum and after a few days of normal eating he returned to his usual non-cannibalistic and not-violent self. .

By week 15 of the 24 week planned starvation period Keys got very worried about the men's psychological deterioration. So he decided to provide a relief meal to boost their morale. It was a great success, although Keys was furious when the men at the end of the meal even ate the orange peel, an item of unknown nutritional and calorific content.

Earl Weygandt was the next to go. First he cheated. He confessed but then kept quiet when his urine looked like it was changing colour. It went from pale, to iced tea colour to beginning to pass blood. He felt guilty, as though he had done it on purpose and he, too, was dropped from the study. The symptoms disappeared when he started eating normally again. So the number of men in the experiment was now reduced by two.

Most of them took cushions with them, wherever they were going as sitting for more than a short time became painful.

Some showed or felt real deterioration. Henry Scholberg got angry with Shakespeare-quoting George Ebeling and told him to shut up. He felt awful remorse and said he was going crazy and felt like he wanted to smash things up. He will reappear in a later chapter, but Keys kept him in. Sam, of the eating alone habit, got so desperate he started to self-harm. He chopped off one of his own fingers with an axe, but he pleaded with Keys to be kept in the study and he was.

'Part of the body's desperate attempt to conserve energy was to lower the thermostat' from 98.6F to 95.8F. The men's heart rates also dropped. During the control phase they were at 55 beats per minute. They dropped to 35 beats per minute and Henry Scholberg dropped to the lowest of just 28 beats per minute.

Around the 20th week of starvation water loss began to plateau mainly because many of the men began to suffer from oedema, water retention, in their legs.

Interestingly, their hearing improved. Unsurprisingly, their co-ordination deteriorated. *How does this link to anorexia?*

Hilde Bruch wrote very clearly that anorectics do not know what hunger is. Interestingly, when she was writing it was not researched very much but, as the search to tackle obesity continues, more money, has been poured into understanding how hunger works, and it is being found to be extremely complicated, with many genes and hormones controlling it.

The men in Keys study volunteered. They were doing so because although being pacifists they wanted to help the war effort in whatever way they could.

We shall think about why anorectics do what they do to themselves in more detail later. But there is a fundamental difference between choosing to do this to yourself and it being done to you. It points in the direction of needing to make sense of an anorectic's experience of it being done to them. Once the anorectic train has run away with them they do not feel as though they have a choice.

For now a sentence or two will suffice. It gives a feeling of control over the self and it narrows the focus. The world of feeling, the world of anxiety, and the question of how to grow up and into the world can be paused. Time can be felt as being stopped, although, of course it isn't. Instead of looking out and scanning the future and possibilities, the eyes and ears are turned inward towards being hungry and how to respond to it. So an anorectic aim is paradoxically to do something damaging to themselves which they view as something helpful. In pursuit of themselves they lose themselves.

As we know, for anorectics hunger is a high. Interestingly, a few of Keys volunteers did continue to restrict their food intake, but most did not. So it is really important to bear in mind that, although there are some common responses to semi-starvation, the anorectic take on it is a particular one. Most of us know we have to eat to live and would not choose to get so dangerously thin.

Remember

If you are anorectic I know that being hungry feels good, extremely good. In fact you are addicted to it. That feeling becomes the solution to everything and that is a problem even if you do not know it is.

CHAPTER V

A Woman's Complicated Relationship with Her Own Body

Birth and the breast

Let us return to that newly born baby bravely making its way across her mother's body to the breast. But hold on, what kind of a mother would give her baby this time? What kind of midwife or husband would trust, would know that a baby could do this?

In the Western world, in good hospitals or home births, the baby is allowed to lie on the mother until the umbilical cord stops beating and is then cut. But this is still rare, more often than not the baby is whisked away, to make sure it is alright, and is then returned to the mother, cleaned up a bit. These are, of course, the circumstances when things go right and not wrong. Birth is a tricky business. Labour can go on for hours. Babies can seem to be reluctant to come into the world and have to be induced, others arrive too soon, and some have difficulty making it through the birth canal, due to size or position and either have to be sucked out with a ventouse, or delivered via caesarean.

Why, you may think, am I telling you about lots of ways of being born? Well, the answer is that all of our experiences create the person that we become and so we need to start at the beginning.

Harry Harlow's famous experiment with monkeys showed that monkeys would rather go towards a soft cuddly toy monkey than a hard one that gave milk. Our skin is our biggest sense organ. Touch is vital in our development and it is how we begin to know where we end and the world, including other people begin. An even starker example is in the rapid reduction of infant mortality due in large part to the practice of kangarooing, where new mothers are encouraged to hold their premature or unwell babies on their bodies, against their skin for as much time as possible. It has produced extraordinary results in reducing infant mortality rates in Ethiopia, particularly for low birth weight babies.

This is in stark contrast to one mother I knew who didn't want to touch her baby at all and when feeding she propped her up on a cushion with a bottle, so that she didn't have to have any physical contact with her baby.

Prematurity

More and more babies, these days survive who in the past would have died. This is a wonderful thing, but it does mean that increasing numbers arrive in the world too soon. Hospitals are much better at allowing parents access. They also increasingly recognize the importance of touch for successful physiological and psychological development. There has not been, as far as I know, any long term research on the link between weight or eating disorders and prematurity. I think there should be. The lack of a womb, the early arrival in the world, the overwhelming stimuli must have an impact on the baby. The question is, of course, what kind of impact it has. It doesn't seem far-fetched to think premature babies might have on-going difficulties making sense of their bodies and the signals they send them.

The importance of touch

Imagine that new born crawling up to her mother's breast. Already she has a sense of taking action on her own behalf. She or he is responding to something inside, and, if all goes according to plan, a satisfying reward awaits. How very different is this from a baby who has a hard birth, or whose cord is cut straightaway, who is picked up, taken off the mother's body, prodded and poked, surrounded by bright lights and noise. That baby is likely to be overwhelmed and simply not able to process things.

You can also think about this story as being about touch. Babies are so vulnerable, and every touch, sound and stimulation or lack of it has an impact on them. How a baby is handled affects them, an extra sensitive, firm but gentle, touch is required at the start. The everyday nature of love and attachment that is shown through touch, whether it is holding hands with a youngster in the street, patting a baby's back to help wind him or her, rocking a baby to sleep in your arms, or stroking or hugging someone to give them comfort.

Donald Winnicott, famously said 'There is no such thing as a baby'. He didn't mean it factually, but rather that where there is a baby there is another person on whom the baby is dependent for survival.

And with touch, this other is not just a pair of arms but a person full of his or her own very strong feelings which will have an impact on the child they are relating to.

Remember, this is not about blame but understanding. This is where some interesting psychoanalytic understanding can come in. As we will discover later, there are so many routes to becoming anorectic, a lot of this is conjecture, so relate to what you read below as a 'pick and mix' opportunity. It may or may not be relevant to the person you are thinking about. These are may bes, not definites.

Melitta Sperling thought that a mother of a baby who went on to develop anorexia had a difficulty seeing her baby as being different from herself. A baby is made inside the body of the mother, and how the mother responds to the baby comes together with the intrinsic character of the baby to influence how it views both itself and the world. You may think what does this mean, not being able to see them as different? This is tricky territory to think about.

Let me give you an example. A young, fragile, anxious girl who is very frightened of life and diets to try and keep her anxiety under control, has a baby. She is terrified when the baby arrives. She is not able to recognise that the baby already has his or her individual identity. She instead just sees another part of herself that she is going to struggle to keep alive. Her baby is treated as a part of her. She assumes the baby is terrified and responds to what she feels when she looks after the baby, rather than responding to the baby herself. So, when she is cold, she puts extra clothes on the baby. This may

be sensible, but the crucial point here is that she uses herself to decide how to respond. She doesn't see and isn't able to hear and respond accurately to the baby in front of her. This is true both physically and emotionally. This leads to a deep down feeling in the baby of still being part of her mother and of not being attended to. Her mother is trying her best, but her own difficulties mean that she and her baby get stuck in a two person dance, or perhaps even a one person dance, as the mother unconsciously plays the tune and the baby has to always follow her moves.

All of this is communicated by touch. The mother's anxiety and tension will be in her hands, her head, her stomach and will impact how she touches, holds, picks-up and responds to her baby.

This particular dance is the key to understanding the difficulties in separating. As the girl grows up, the only way she knows how to get some of her needs met is to become more and more attuned to what is going on in her mother. I shall look at a clinical example which Gianna Williams writes about later where the mother uses the baby for her own psychic survival.

This leads, for some, to not knowing how to be different

from their mother. They have to try and assert themselves and so they turn to the only thing they feel they have control over, that is their body. Emotionally they are unformed, they don't know what they feel, how to feel or how to speak, and yet they desperately want to let people know they need some space and time to grow and to point out that they are not alright.

This crisis often comes at adolescence when a move into the world away from home is expected. When a woman who knows so little of herself is suddenly asked to function as an adult, this so often leads to an unconscious 'No'. The body seems to be saying 'I simply cannot cope with this'.

The body has not had a chance to learn how to function. The body is where and how we feel, not the mind. We have to feel enough at home in our skins before we can relate to another's body and so the advent of adolescence can be terrifying with its bodily changes and hormonal surges which for an anorectic is asking too much.

Anorexia and sex part one

A common idea about anorexia is that it is a retreat from womanhood. This is true. The body of a woman without the normal sexual characteristics of breasts, hips and thighs obviously looks pre-pubescent. There is a healthy pre-pubescent look and the agonizingly thin look of an anorectic.

Yet, some anorectic women do have sex. I find it problematic that anyone would want to have sex with someone who is so fragile emotionally and physically. Some people do, but when you talk to anorectics who have had sex when they are very thin, they are often not psychologically present; they try and get as far away from their body as they possibly can. They often, in fact, dissociate. There are different ways this happens but one is to experience yourself as quite outside of your body, often watching it from above.

As we have seen in the chapter on hunger, anorectics are frightened of their own appetite, and this can include their sexual appetite. They are frightened that like their hunger it may grab them and they may rip through the world in a sexual frenzy. Once again, this may be a very deeply buried worry which may be quite inaccessible to them.

There is a desire to know

In the United Kingdom we have one of the highest rate of teenage pregnancies in Europe. Research shows the more sex education that children have, the lower the rate of unwanted pregnancies. Not having your period is a sure fire way not to become pregnant. But it is not only anorectics who want to know about their own and others sexuality. Most girls have very little help working out what is going on in their bodies. Our culture in the West has gone somewhat sex mad. Sexual abuse is an awful thing and should not happen, but behaving as though a girl's body is dangerous because some troubled man cannot control his own need for power through sex misses the point. The only way that that young girl is going to become empowered is through understanding and knowing about her own body. She has to be confident enough to know what sex is, if she wants it and who with. Men have to deal with their own role in this.

This sexualisation of a woman's body is damaging to women and society. A woman's body is about more than her sexuality. It is the home of her heart and her very being. It deserves love, attention and care. Even writing like this feels strange, for women are so used to looking at their bodies with critical eyes. Whose those eyes are will vary, but they are rarely compassionate and often viciously critical and impossibly demanding.

Kim Chernin writes beautifully in her book *The Hungry Self: Women, Eating and Identity* about how both girls and boys start off discovering their own bodies. Think of a baby lying on the floor delighting in finding her feet, or discovering that a hand put here or there can make a shadow or stop a ray of light.

A body can sometimes make our wishes come true. We learn to eat, to move, to walk and to talk. We discover agency as we discover ourselves. This includes using our mouths to talk and eat with, our hands to explore ourselves and others.

A secure body image develops when we are supported in finding out how our own body works and how it relates to another. You don't get an idea of your own boundaries, your own skin unless you rub up against someone else's. That is what helps define ourselves to ourselves.

Children have sexual feelings and desires, although, as with so much else in life there is a continuum from those children who have a strong sex drive to those who have a very weak one. How parents respond to their child's body, from birth onwards, has an impact on their son or daughter.

Often parents feelings about their child are mediated through their own internal judgements that they make towards themselves. A mother who hates her body is likely to have difficulty with her daughter's body as well.

This is before the issue of sex itself comes onto the scene.

Hopefully, you will have some sense of how complicated

every woman's relationship with her body is. An anorectics is even more so.

I remember one anorectic young woman, a member of the audience, when I was giving a talk on eating disorders, and I touched on the subject of sex. She was furious. She said no one ever talked about it with her and she wanted to know why. She said it was really important. I quite agree. Desire and appetite and their close to total repression are vital components of anorexia. What lies behind the repression of desire?

I shall deal with this from one angle in the chapter on 'Inside the Mind of an Anorectic', but as so much of the difficulty of the anorectic mind lies in problems of the body and what it does and how it functions I have decided that I am going to deal with the nitty gritty question of sex in more detail here.

One woman, abused by someone who worked for her parents, saw them talking to him years later, and she was very frightened and remembered telling her friend 'I think he's telling them what a naughty girl I am'. She assumed she was the dangerous one. No-one had really talked to her about her body, about sensuality, sexuality, about her own body boundaries and how to protect herself. If as a child you have knowledge of yourself and how your body works you are going to be in a much better position to say 'no' to anyone who behaves inappropriately towards you.

You are, of course, going to need to know about the whole range of feelings you have and what they signal and mean for you, not just sexual ones.

Anorexia and sex part two

These facts are basic. Sex can lead to pregnancy, and pregnancy can lead to the birth of a baby. A baby needs to be looked after and fed and to be brought up and so the whole circle starts again. Death is somewhere in this circuit too, and there are a number of things about this whole process that are close to intolerable for an anorectic young woman.

One of the things I really want to do in this book is to show you how apparently nonsensical, powerful forces inside us can structure how we behave, with us barely realising it. If you ask a woman with anorexia if she can imagine being a mother, the answer is almost always 'no'.

What might she be frightened of ? For the moment let us focus on her body. I am going to use Claire as an example here. This doesn't mean everyone who is anorectic has these particular fears but they may have them in some way or another.

Claire

Claire had stages when she did everything she could to keep me out. What she told me about her fears of being pregnant, about what happened to a mother's body, about her own total bewilderment, about procreation and the process of birth, all came from the time after she had let me in. She would tell me, whilst in great discomfort and with much difficulty, how she simply couldn't believe that a baby could come out of a woman's vagina. She believed it would kill the woman, like a watermelon bursting on the ground, she would be irreparably damaged. The idea of having a baby felt dangerous and damaging. She did not believe that her own body would survive.

She had a friend who did survive having a daughter. This little girl's name was Bonnie, and Claire, who was a good friend, often helped look after her. Bonnie's mother became pregnant again and Bonnie was told she was going to have a little brother or sister. Claire gave Bonnie a bath one night. Bonnie used the soap as a pretend baby. She would pick up the soap, pretend she had a big tummy, crouch down and produce the bar of soap baby over and over and over again. Claire found it hard to tolerate and very hard to sit with, but she did. It was as though

Bonnie was showing her what she needed to do. To manage

something you have to go over and over it until it makes sense. Claire realised with great sadness that no one had ever told her about what would happen to her body as she grew up. No-one had helped her to trust that she could play, experiment and be in her own skin. This meant she didn't know about growing breasts, having periods, what sex was, what it meant and where it might lead. She began to be a little bit interested in her body and how it worked. For the first time, thanks to her very small friend, she began to believe it could work.

Claire feared childbirth was damaging. Deep down she believed she had damaged her mother by being born.

Fat and anorexia

Claire's example of not knowing about periods and her own body is one reason why she might have chosen to retreat from womanhood. Fat is quintessentially connected to feminity. You need a certain percentage of fat to have periods, regardless of your BMI. Attempts to quantify this have failed, probably because every person's body is different, but what is certain is that for every woman there is a point at which losing fat will lead to her having irregular or non-existent periods.

So the irrational fear of fat that an anorectic has can be thought of, in part, as a desire not to grow into a woman.

Fat is also disturbing because it is associated with softness, comfort, vulnerability and lack of control. By lack of control, I mean that fat on a body moves, wobbles, and takes up space. All these things are disturbing for anorectics. If they look fat, they are, in their own minds clearly demonstrating that they have an appetite, that they desire things and that they are meeting some of their own needs. This is not to happen. However, fat is vital for life and is valuable. Women can't have children without it. It makes up 20% of everyone's brain and is soft and comforting and comfortable.

Does an anorectic misperceive her body?

Misperceptions by anorectics of their bodies being fat when they are not are one of the things that tend not to be on the list of anorectic attributes these days. However, it is increasingly understood that anorectics tend to look and feel most acutely aware of any fat on their body and hate it. They only focus on the parts they want to get rid of, so they say they are fat because they have some fat on them. They hate fat. As Elizabeth said, 'My self-image was that I was thinnish but still had pockets of 'fat' which I wanted gone. The tidiness of this form of self-hatred is very neat. The thing that I hate and which bothers me

is now under my control and I can attack it and make it die

in front of my eyes'. This is problematic.

What is not in this chapter

It is so complicated, for everyone, to be able to know that the emotions they have take place inside their body and need to be experienced and named, if life is to be negotiated successfully. I have given you a glimpse of what I mean by sharing the example of Claire and her witnessing Bonnie work out where babies come from. The hard part is to recognise that we need to experience all of the basic emotions of love, rage, grief and guilt that we have inside, before we can feel safe in the world. This process is too complex to try and describe for each and every feeling, but even having a vague idea of what I mean, may be of some use. When we are not able to differentiate our feelings and do not know how to have them, our bodies respond by becoming chronically anxious in one way or another. For, once you know you can have a feeling, survive and not instantly act on it, you have choice. We are talking deep down strong, primitive, powerful feelings here, not your everyday ones This is where real self-esteem comes from. It comes from the inside out, not the outside in.

Crucially, the only way you can feel your feelings is in and through your body, not in your mind. So an anorectic, by stopping her body functioning , is trying to stop having to feel. This doesn't mean she doesn't feel at all, but it is rather muted. In common with Claire, many anorectics feelings get redirected towards resisting eating surviving in their diminished state and keeping others away. In fact, there is little room left for these individuals to 'be themselves', however, corny that may sound. If you cut yourself off from your core feelings, you lose access to them all, this means loving feelings are lost, as well as angry, scary and painful ones. For an anorectic, a diminished body means having a diminished heart and a restricted mind.

From the inside and from the outside

Social media encourages an external evaluation of the self. These means my life may be evaluated by myself according to how I appear on FaceBook. How you look on the outside can become the sole test of being ok. This is problematic for many. How we feel, should come from the inside out, not from the outside in. How do you feel in your body as you are reading this? Are you sitting comfortably? Where are you? What are you aware of in your body? Its temperature, its comfort, its discomfort. Do you feel generally good or bad? Now do the same if you think of someone taking a photograph of you.

I bet you instantly pull your stomach in, or move to show

some bit of you that you like, or to hide some bit of you that you don't. This doesn't tend to help self confidence and self-esteem does it?

It reminds me of a body image study where a woman had a pretend, not very pretty, scar put on her cheek and she was sent into a cocktail party and asked to notice how people responded to her. When she came out she was asked how it went and she said it was awful, that people kept on looking at that side of her face, and she found it really difficult. They held up a mirror to her. They hadn't put anything on her face at all.

So it is complicated. How we think we look has a real bearing on how we feel and then on to how we behave with others. We can then imagine that they respond in a certain way, although there is no knowing if this woman kept touching her face, or behaving in such a way that she drew attention to herself. What is difficult for women who are not anorectic to realise is that an anorectic believes that she looks fine. That is what denial means. It may occasionally be punctured, but when it is in full flow they simply cannot understand why people are making such a fuss about them.

How anorexia attempts to by-pass the body

Anorexia is not caused by dieting. When you talk to women who are anorectic, or who have been, a very complicated story comes out, usually at core about an environment where they had no idea what was going on inside of themselves and had no capacity to work it out. This is exactly what Hilde Bruch found. That these women were in a blur about the information their bodies gave them. This will be explored in more depth in the chapter: 'Inside the Mind of an Anorectic'

What might an anorectic body be saying?

If we give the anorectic body words perhaps it is saying, 'I don't know how to be'. This is just the start. Keep reading to find out more.

Remember

You cannot live without your body.

Chapter VI

If Self- Starvation is the Answer, What is the Question?

Lynn Crilly in her book, speaks about how awful it was when she was told that her daughter's anorexia was her fault. Janet Treasure clearly states that it is not the fault of the parents. I wholeheartedly agree, and what I am going to say next is not going to contradict this very important fact. As a parent it is not your fault. How we become the human beings we are is a profoundly complicated question. As you will have read in the chapter on eating, we start off in the womb with different feelings, behaviours and predilections. Do you blame the twin who was keen on licking in the womb, and then loved eating, on her parents because they conceived her? How far back in time do you go? There is also the impact of the environment. I would say that how a person becomes the person they are is a complicated, exquisite, sometimes painful dance between their genetic inheritance and their experiences. Their experiences take place in their environment, and within this are the important figures of their parents, carers and siblings.

As a parent it is not your fault, but who you are will have had an impact on your daughter.

At some point what happens next is up to them. How anyone takes a look, a stroke, a word, a sentence is a very complex matter. If you are the parent and are reading this, it is not your fault, but in your child's mind, deep down it might be. This is the crux of the matter. It is also an opportunity. For if your child can be helped to learn how to have a feeling, to recognise what it is, to understand the reasons she has avoided them for so long and how she does this, then she can begin to change. Eating disorders do not have to be a life sentence. As a parent you may not have known how to separate from your daughter, and you may not know how to do the things I have just described for yourself. Recognising your own limits and seeking help to grow yourself is always wise. Being a parent of an anorectic is really tough.

What you see is what you get, part one

Anorexia is a bodily response to something that cannot be communicated as effectively in any other way. Although there are, of course, the immediate triggers, there remains a mystery at the core. The original cover I wanted for the book didn't come out as I had imagined and hoped but it still remains alive in my mind. A woman, an anorectic woman, sits with her head in her hands, in a room that could be a prison. There is a light coming in through a very small skylight high up in a corner, warm and dusty, shining on the floor a few feet from her. This in some ways says it all. An anorectic is in despair, in private, not in public. Her anorexia is a prison, a self imposed prison that she has no idea she can escape from. There is hope but she won't and can't see it. In fact, she cannot even raise her head out of her hands to look about her. Now, what on earth, can this possibly be a solution to? I am a fan of this image. It was told to me by more than one anorectic verbally, and painted by another in an art therapy group, and for me it communicates the complexity of what lies ahead.

So what is the question that self-starvation is the answer to?

There are a number of precursors to becoming anorectic. A particular capacity to focus is thought to be one contributing factor. Another is depression, where interestingly the mind tends to see the world as unchanging and stuck in a more global sense, so that the possibility of change in the details is avoided. It is important to remember that the woman who suffers from anorexia is aware, at least tangentially, of the message she wants to send. One of the first things anorexia does is taking over. It is preoccupying to a massive degree. It takes time, energy, emotion and determination. If you have ever got very, very tired and had to keep going, you will know the feeling of being present and not being present at the same time. Something similar happens when you are anorectic. You become so attuned to the hunger and the constant pain that your body is in that there is no space for you to interact with your own feelings. As we have already seen this capacity to ignore the self is disastrous if the individual is to recover.

The obvious question is why the woman with anorexia is so keen to avoid herself ? The reasons are multiple, but in essence it is because she is terrified. She is terrified of who she is and what she might feel if she allows herself to. Yet, she really doesn't know this. The tangential awareness I mention is like seeing something out of the corner of your eye, but never being able to see it properly.

But she shows us. She shows us her capacity to damage by how she is hurting herself. She is terrified of how she can hurt others and the feelings that she would have if she lets herself know how hurt she is. How and why this comes about is different for everyone, but I shall give a few of the possible routes that lead to an anorectic destination. I am starting with the final trigger, because it is the easiest to answer.

The final trigger

The final, final trigger is often a diet that works, so that people notice and say things like 'You look really good' or 'How have you managed to lose so much weight?' The answer is quite simple, by not eating so much, and so the young woman thinks, as a method of gaining attention this works. To me this is always problematic, as it usually means other women supporting an aesthetic which is explicitly communicating that you looked worse when you weighed more. There is a whole potential book on fattism here and its pernicious hold on women and men. There will be more on this in *C is For Compulsive Eating*.

However, it is also true that in the Western world a very high percentage of women diet all the time, whether through calorie controlled ones, ultra healthy ones, ultra limited and unhealthy ones, and yet the majority of these women do not end up anorectic, so what is it about those that do?

If you asked an anorectic whilst she was anorectic what triggered her to become so, her answer would most likely be that it was a diet that went wrong. That is, indeed, what many of the experts such as Janet Treasure say, too. But this still leaves the question of why doesn't everyone who diets become anorectic?

If, on the other hand you ask parents when they think it started, or you do a timeline of the young person's life, you will often find the start coincides with an external event, such as the loss of a relationship through relocation, rejection or death.

If you ask the anorectic themselves they are not likely to have any idea. It is only when they have recovered that they will be likely and able to answer you differently. If they were able to answer the question they probably wouldn't be anorectic in the first place.

What leads to the final trigger?

What you don't see on the cover is the anorectic herself. I want to return to Violet and the unwrapped mummy in the British Museum, or any other starving body that comes to mind. What do you see and what do you feel? When I see people that thin, I feel shocked. I think how can someone treat another human being like that? I think how skeletal, how asexual, how diminished, how fragile and how close to death the person looks. There is no doubt they have a problem. It makes me want to scream at them. Why are you doing this to yourself?

When a person does this to themselves, they are yelling with their bodies that they have a problem. They are silently screaming. Their body is trying to speak what is unspeakable and trying to show that it knows what is unknowable. A choice is being made. It is an unconscious choice, which has to be known and understood before change can happen and be sustained. If the individual knew the reason why they were doing what they are doing to themselves they could have more say in stopping it As one woman said to me 'I didn't know, I didn't understand. My body was trying to tell me and other people something was wrong. I hurt myself. I didn't know I was hurting.'. So what kind of hurting is going on? One answer is that it is a response to loss. To understand loss you need first to understand identification.

Identification instead of separation

Mara Selvini Palazzoli, a family therapist, thought that anorectics were unable to know that their body was their own. They took in how, usually, their mother had behaved towards them as though they still remained a part of her. So their focus was always towards keeping the other ok in order to look after themselves. Then in a desperate attempt to separate they would starve themselves in order to try to find themselves. They were hoping to starve the mother out of them, without realising they could not do that without starving themselves in the process. This is similar to Melitta Sperling, who I mentioned earlier and who saw much of the problem as being that the mother believed the child to be an extension of herself, almost like an actual, rather than metaphorical right arm. This can also be true of fathers. It makes the task of psychic separation for the child inconceivable. When you are totally part of something, even having an idea that something else is possible is impossible. It is rather like two balls of string being seamlessly connected, and then being asked to pull them apart, when you cannot even see where they were joined. This links to many other psychoanalytic thinkers who found that fragile parents ask, without realising it, for their children to emotionally take care of them rather than the other way around.

In other words, this is where the mother unconsciously identifies with her child in a way that allows her no sense of having a separate boundary, a separate skin. This is an unhealthy form of identification. It has a healthy and normal aspect which I am going to describe now.

Normal identification

Identification is a normal part of growing up. One toddler without realising it walks like her father, another has a very similar posture to her mother. Genetics, to one side, this is often simply an unconscious connection through taking in and imitating at a deep level the people around you. It is part of a wider process of how you take in the world. It has a particularly powerful role in adolescence. It occupies a strange space between two worlds. The adolescent adoration of pop stars, film stars, musicians or YouTubers often leads to them adopting an element of them for themselves. This might be a pair of shoes, an expression, mannerisms, a haircut, and often it happens because the individual is engrossed by the other. They do not think consciously, 'I will wear shoes like them because I like them'. The process is rather that they find when they go to buy a pair of shoes they are simply drawn to them. This means they end up wearing shoes just like the person they adore. This is a process of attachment and love of a kind. It does and is meant to show the strong emotional identification between the star and his or her fan. This doesn't, of course, just occur in adolescence, but goes on throughout our lives. As we grow up we find other ways to take in and attach to people, not only by being like them, but it does remain a part of us.

Bereavement

This process of identification seems particularly true for a number of anorectics in relation to bereavement. Many people stop eating in response to a loved one dying. Their body shuts down, they go into shock. They no longer want to live. Yet this phase passes. But for some women, already struggling with being separate from their parents, it can be too much to bear. One woman I know became anorectic in response to the death of her grandfather. She became a dying body to show the distress that she was unable to feel and know. She was simultaneously and unconsciously protesting about the loss by identifying with her grandfather, rather than being able to mourn him. Loss in adolescence, when you are on the verge of adult life, is profoundly shocking and sometimes the body seems to simply respond before any emotional digestion is able to take place. Another woman lost the nanny she loved, quite unexpectedly. She died. She was her *de facto* mother. She lost weight, retreated from puberty and took up a body, an asexual body, that was similar to the woman's she'd loved. As always with the unconscious the meanings are multiple. There is a clue in their retreat from life as they lose weight, but also a desire to keep and remain close to the person they have loved.

Other types of loss

Ellen West's eating disorder seems to have been triggered by the break-up of a relationship, a relationship not ended by the student she had fallen for or by her but by her father. Emma Wolf, whose lover broke up with her by email, writes, 'I went completely blank, I couldn't get my mind around living without him. Then I took a shower, unlocked the door and set about destroying myself '. What is not experienced in these examples is the process of grief and grieving-the process whereby feelings have to be had, over and over again and survived.

Core difficulties

Emma Wolf and Janet Treasure both talk about anorectics being super-sensitive to rejection, prone to depression and having very low self-esteem. When talking about why, it is not so much chicken and egg but rather that, if as both Gianna Williams and Marilyn Lawrence in their different ways suggest, a woman who goes on to develop anorexia feels persecuted, then starving is a way of trying to control and manage an unmanageable part of herself. As we have seen in the chapter on hunger she is frightened of her appetite. She is also very frightened of what she feels. This leads to deeper and deeper attempts to deny self-knowledge and the feelings inside her which she experiences as increasingly dangerous as they are pushed further and further down. As Elizabeth said to me 'Getting thin was a way of protecting people from how dangerous I was'. The anorectic becomes more and more omnipotent in order to survive. This means denying more and more profoundly how at risk her life may be becoming. The knowledge of there being anything in the world which is not in her possession and control feels unbearable. Instead 'less' becomes 'more'; to avoid wanting becomes the clue to existence. This, of course, leads to a very barren and limited life. Often an anorectic will behave as though people and food are of no use to her now and never have been.

This means change of any kind is very hard to manage as it often stirs up an unwanted awareness of dependence. One kind of change that often occurs for a child is the arrival of a sibling.

Siblings

Just as death and loss are shocking and change our worlds; so too is birth. No mother can ever prepare for birth. You cannot know how you are going to be and what is going to happen until it happens. But as a mother you have some choice about becoming pregnant, about having sex and knowing in theory what will happen. If you are a child of a mother who has another child it is a very different situation. We know the brains of mothers and fathers change in response to having a child, particularly a first child. Often parents who are somewhat vulnerable fall in love with their child in a way which catches them entirely by surprise. This may be because their own beginnings were shaky and, without realising it, they find the love in themselves for their new born which they wish they had been on the receiving end of.

So they cherish, adore, respond to their daughter, meet her every whim, try and protect her from every nasty thing out there in the world, and she is the apple of their eye and then... someone else appears. For some this outrageous displacement cannot be recovered from. They feel unloved, unwanted, and furious. Parents have to know and facilitate the expression of hate to lance it in their first born. I remember one child thrillingly playing with a castle and endlessly pouring hot oil onto her enemies, who were led by her newly arrived sister, a monster baby general.

Clichéd though it is, it is true. Anger that cannot be known, experienced and tolerated, turns with a horrible viciousness upon the person who has it. Some people never recover from the birth of a sibling. They find many different routes to express their distress. One of them may be by becoming anorectic. This is more likely if they are already struggling with the hard task we all have of making sense of the world.

Clinical example

Claire had a sister. I often forgot she did. Claire needed my full attention and she got it. Her rage which almost stopped us from working together (see the next chapter) continued to appear understandably and episodically. The last momentous occasion was when I went on maternity leave. This is awful for people who see therapists. Unlike most other situations you never get to see the rival you had such strong feelings about, and you really are abandoned, usually for quite a few months. I was away looking after my new baby, and Claire was hurt and cross. After a lot of discussion we had decided together that she would see another therapist whilst I was away and come back to me when I returned to work. About two months into my maternity leave a letter appeared in the post. It was addressed to 'Em Farrell (therapist)'. I opened it and found a pretty card inside. Inside the card was a hand-written poem. It was written in black and red ink. The words in black described a baby who was sitting happily on my lap. The words in red ink were images of violent attacks on my body and the baby's. I didn't keep the card. In retrospect I think the word therapist on the envelope was a warning to me, the mother, to watch out. I hadn't heeded it, though, and shock shot through me.

Claire gave me a beautiful star she made of clay and a flourishing plant in a woven basket when we finished working together a couple of years later. She now has two lovely boys of her own. She will, I am sure, have helped her first son with his feelings about the arrival of the second. These feelings, if accepted and felt can then make way for other loving ones. They are part of growing and becoming. This means speaking, playing and feeling, not ranting and taking action.

The clarity of the anorectic communication

As we have already seen in the chapters on Hunger and The Body, how people develop is extremely complicated and individuaistic. Hilde Bruch's research suggests that when someone is anorectic they are unable to make sense of their body. This is crucial in understanding its strange role in the illness and in indicating the direction of interventions that are needed if you are going to help someone get out of it. The extent of the denial is very powerful and once again we are talking about deep down intractable denial. As Eric, one of Hilde Bruch's patient said on getting a new job, 'Why is my face so red and why are my hands so wet?' He had no capacity to observe his physical sensations of anxiety and make sense of them. There is a lot of work to do. As years of feelings remain locked inside without being understood, known or experienced, the danger feels twofold. It could potentially come from the unknown inside and/or the unknown outside.

Inside the anorectic feels tiny, dangerous and worried, all without being very conscious of it.

Trans-generational transmission of trauma

This is painful and sometimes true. Grandparents who survived being in concentration camps now have granddaughters who look like they have just been released from one. As so often with unconscious non-verbal communication the answer lies right in front of them. What happened to them needs to be voiced. There is pain that goes back generations, pain that is thought to be unbearable that has been sidestepped in an attempt to live, but has without words been carried down into

the next generation and beyond. Beginning to acknowledge
and speak about what happened can change things.

What is anorexia an answer to?

At core it is a way to avoid having to feel and know about
yourself, your needs, your wishes, your abilities, your mistakes.
These things are very, very frightening. The level of rage
is volcanic in response to hurt and loss if it is not felt and
processed. Like a boomerang, it is simply redirected towards
the self. As Emma Wolf said, she set about destroying herself.
She punished herself, instead of allowing herself to feel her
anger, her guilt about her destructive wishes and her grief for
herself and the relationship. Her anorexia short-circuited the
process of moving forward and, instead, seemed to try and
stop time.

It is usually more than a growing up problem

I remember having my own difficulties with depression in
my late teens. I went to see lovely Dr. Rowntree, long since
sadly deceased. He told me that he woke up feeling depressed,
every morning. He said that once he had got up and got going
he was fine. He must have been in his late 60s at the time, and
I remember feeling both shocked and relieved that someone
who seemed so well, who worked hard and who seemed so

full of life was identifying with, rather than dismissing me. As I explained my difficulties he said 'It sounds like a growing up problem to me'. He had hit the nail on the head.

Anorexia can be thought of as an extreme variant of this. If anorexia starts during teenage years then the body of an anorectic goes from having female womanly characteristics, to becoming pre-pubescent looking, to if things get very bad, barely human at all. So we can think of anorexia as a potentially dangerous regression. It is a problem of how to negotiate life. I was stuck and didn't know how to move forward. For anorectics who have it badly, they seem to be running backwards towards smallness and death, rather than forwards and growing into their own lives. We'll look at this in more depth in the next chapter where we'll take the thought of going backwards in order to try and go forwards seriously.

Remember and...

Which of the above makes sense to you? Write down the triggers, from the final to the first. If there is a trigger that I have missed please let me know.

CHAPTER VII

Inside the Mind and of an Anorectic

A s I have already said, I wanted a picture of an anorectic woman on the front cover. I hoped it would work, but it didn't. I googled images of anorexia and was shocked. Some of the pictures looked like the walking dead. If you go to Wikipedia and look up the history of anorexia, there are photographs take an of an anorectic woman whom I suspect had been paraded naked in front of students at the Salpêtrière, as was the custom. Yet again I found myself thinking 'how can such a thin body survive?' This at times links to bereavement again. There can be a forceful denial of the reality of death. They, unlike the rest of us, can survive with eating barely anything for years. Some are in their own minds close to immortal. Their body is insubstantial and the hope and the idea is that their mind, which so imprisons them, really doesn't need nutrition. This is not good news. Some psychoanalysts think an anorectic believes she is still inside the womb and so doesn't need to eat as she is still being fed by mother.

Does an anorectic intend to die?

We are talking here about anorectics whose anorexia has run with them for a long time, when they no longer have any memory that it was an answer to a question. It is now simply an inescapable way of life.

The death rate of anorexia is high and many early workers such as Charcot and Janet believed anorectics did want to die. Anorectics die for two reasons. One is through actively taking their own life, and the second is through the consequences of starvation on the body. It begins to shut down, turn on itself and becomes more vulnerable to infection and collapse. Being anorectic is desperately isolating, lonely and sad, and some people simply cannot bear it. They lose any sense of hope and are under the false impression that their death will make it easier for those they love.

There are reasons to consider why what appears to be death-seeking may not always be. A common delusion is that they are superhuman. Unlike the rest of us they do not need food to survive. They can manage without. They want to get rid of their body without getting rid of their mind. This is a problem.

Thinking about saying 'No'

An anorectic cannot, will not, does not, know how to turn towards the light, even when it is in the same room as her. Gianna Williams, author *of Internal Landscapes and Foreign Bodies: Eating Disorders and Other Pathologies,* calls it the 'no entry' syndrome. Sometimes the NO is very strong indeed. I remember one young woman. She came into my consulting room and didn't sit down. She stood with her back to me. The session was 50 minutes. She was a teenager and she did not speak. I spoke now and then, saying rather obvious things like 'You seem very angry about being here and clearly don't want to speak to me'. I would then venture a few tentative ideas as to why that might be. She came three times and spoke two sentences. That was it. She was then taken away by her parents to a residential unit. My overriding impression of that young girl was that she was furious at being brought to see me. She didn't want help, and the best I could do was to hear her 'No'.

Gianna William's example was of a much less obvious 'No'. She tracked her patient's reluctance to allowing her in to the experience she had of a mother who needed her daughter to mother her in ways she could not manage. This is so important when thinking about anorexia. It is not a game of blame but there is no doubt that how the families we arrive in, the people who bring us up and the environment we inhabit impact us all. This is in addition to what we are born with. Parenting that goes well helps the parts of us that need help negotiate with difficult things inside of us. This in turn helps us to relate as well as we can to what is outside of us.

So, coming back to Gianna Williams' patient. Gianna first saw Sally when she was a worrying thin 17 year old. She was of Afro-Caribbean origin, and her mother had been a very, very anxious woman. She was so frightened of having a bath, due to her own early trauma, that she had to have her daughter sit beside and hold her hand. So from a young age Sally was her mother's helper. She was given the responsibility of holding the anxiety and feelings that her mother could not.

Once again, let me say, this is not about blaming the mother. This mother loved her daughter as best she could, but this did not mean that her own difficulties did not impact her to such a degree that she had to ask her daughter to help her. The only problem with it was that her daughter was too young to manage the level of anxiety her mother gave her, which meant she had very little chance to understand, know about or process her own. Poor Sally's mother died when Sally was only

13. She had been anorectic too, and was terrified all the time, unless she was drunk.

This circuit of cumulative trauma was awful for Sally. There was no room or help to process her own feelings, let alone her feelings about her mother so she had to find some way to save herself. Putting up a wall to stop things from coming in, was, at least, a beginning. Of course, sadly, the wall stopped good and nourishing food and feelings from coming in, as well as difficult and overwhelming ones.

Anorectics come with all sorts of differences, but they chose a similar route to express their distress and try to tell us and themselves something important about themselves.

Trying to make sense of the non-verbal messages

What is, of course, true is that an anorectic treats her body very badly, and once again, this provides a clue. It is designed to show us in some way how she feels she has been treated. If you really want to understand anorexia you need to attend with exquisite care and detail to the person in front of you and their experience. She hurts herself and is cruel to herself and, if these aspects of her were present before the start of the anorexia, then we have another way of making sense of the self-starvation. It may be a way of continuing a trend of self harm that she has practiced for a long time in her mind.

And it ends with it running away with her. As Sharon, another of Hilde Bruch's patients said, about her own relationship to not eating, in that she behaved towards herself 'the way inmates in a concentration camp would surrender to brutal guards'. As Hilde Bruch said, she behaved 'as if she were a compulsively driven robot'.

Importance of internal passivity

What is crucial is that many anorectics do behave like robots. Marilyn Charles wrote about her work with a badly anorectic woman and made the spot-on point that it was as though her patient had no idea that she needed to develop. There is, as you can see, in the quote above, no hint that Sharon had any say in what happened in her own mind. This is very normal. The train has run away with her and the link to the fact that she not only made the train, but some part of her is driving it - has got entirely lost.

The anorectic mind I got to know best

So I am going to take you into the room on the cover,-the prison that keeps people out and doesn't even allow them to look at the available light. I am going do this through talking about Claire. Hers is the anorectic mind that I know best. She taught me so much and I will always be in her debt for that.

I saw her three times a week for some ten years. The notes I kept on her have long since been shredded, so what I am drawing on is my memory of our work together. This will mean in practice I don't know that she will recognise herself. My memory for facts has never been too good, but for feelings it is, and that is how I am going to try to reconstruct some more of our time together. So for now I am going back to where we started.

She was unusual. She was the first anorectic who self-referred when I set up a Centre for Women with Eating Disorders. Bulimic women flooded in, some of whom were recovering anorectics. But in came Claire, suspicious, very thin and quite hostile, looking around the room as though something was bound to attack her. She was definitely anorectic and had come of her own volition. This in itself is rare. She made it clear in the first session that she had had a lot of help and she doubted that I would have anything useful to give her. 'What did I know about anorexia?'

I said I knew something about it, but that she knew a lot more than I did, and if she wanted me to help she'd have to tell me about it. I said I didn't know whether I would be able to help but that I would be willing to give it a go if she was.

This wasn't and isn't my normal stance with people that I see, but her level of hostility made me realise that I needed to get permission to join her in her anorectic space, her anorectic prison. When I owned up to not knowing she visibly relaxed, just a fraction. She always sat right on the edge of the seat, and always said how uncomfortable my chairs were. I moved three times during my years of working with her and thought of her when buying or changing chairs. There was a wicker one with a cushion, that I remember really liking. She always said my chairs were designed to be so uncomfortable that after 50 minutes, the length of her session, you'd want to leave. In effect, the self-ejecting therapy chairs. Everything seemed to conspire to get rid of her.

She was living with her mother when she first came to see me. I have little recollection of her father. He featured much more later on, as she began to recover. She was in her early twenties and was not able to work. She was very thin and often looked very cold. She didn't wear very baggy clothes, so I could see her shape. She gave me the sense of being and feeling hard and desperate. As my memories of her reappear and I think of her bright intense eyes. I feel full of anxiety and love.

We focused on the present, not the past. The question was how she was going to create a life that she could bear to live in. She wanted to move away from home, but only saw herself becoming homeless and living on the street, as though that was the only alternative.

Coming back to my own shorthand when giving talks on anorexia, the two words on the whiteboard used to be 'sex' and 'separation'. Claire taught me a lot about these topics and I will start with separation.

My sense of our work in the early days was about building trust. I had no idea how it was going or where we were heading. She came and we tried to make sense of things together. It was her responses to the breaks in the work that worried me and got me thinking. She got angry before they happened, often very angry. She would say she might not come back, covertly threatening suicide. The loss was too much for her to bear. On returning from one break she told me she had laid sharp knives out on her bed. I had the image of her attacking herself with them. She told me that when she had been hospitalised for anorexia, which she had hated, she had got into a fight with some nurses. She had physically held off four of them for quite a long period of time. I said she wanted me to know not only how incredibly angry she was, but that I should be worried for myself, that she was very strong and that if she wanted to hurt me she would be able to. Once again it was very important to take her communication seriously, to hear it, and for her to know that I had really understood it.

And she did hurt me, not physically, but emotionally. In retrospect, stage one corresponds to consulting room one, where our relationship slowly got established. Stage two equates with consulting room two, where her rage and hate came to the fore and stayed there. The move from consulting room one to consulting room two seemed to stop any communication other than anger and despair. I remember thinking that nothing that I did or said was right. There was a computer in the room, and I remember her saying she wanted to smash it. It sat just to my left. I felt useless as a therapist, that I had nothing to offer her, that I could not help. She was furious with me for this being true. I panicked when I was with her. Often I didn't know how I would get through the session. I held on to what a supervisor once said to a supervisee, that sometimes all you can do is hold on to the arms of the chair.

I wished she'd used the couch, so that I didn't have to be

so directly in her firing line. She could see her bullets hitting home though. I was anxious, defeated and worried by the end of sessions with her. I went to supervision. My supervisor tried to help but she didn't seem to be able to reach me. I read everything I could find to try and hold myself together. That didn't help either. My supervisor suggested that I should stop working with her, that she couldn't make use of therapy. The subtext was that she was clearly damaging my confidence as well. Claire had clearly read my mind and said she couldn't see the point of continuing coming to see me as I was of no help. I with some element of relief and some of sadness, said ok and we made a decision to end. It was a few weeks off as, in good psychoanalytic tradition, I had allowed some time for our ending. I do remember thinking that I was perhaps simply being a masochist by prolonging our relationship that seemed to be causing us both pain. I think I would be much better equipped to deal with her raw feelings now, but I was quite young then and had not worked as a therapist for that long. Now I think I would be quicker to recognise what was right in front of me. She could not bear to need me or indeed anyone so much.

As I struggled through that final session I was acutely aware of how little I knew about Claire. She was cross. That much was clear, and she wasn't eating enough to keep her body and mind together, but her anger so filled the sessions that there was no room for any other form of connection. She felt so angry with me for not giving her what she wanted. Although, I don't think either of us knew what it was that she wanted. All the therapy was about was our relationship and how it had failed her. In the world of therapy there is the idea that a person brings their deepest, most embedded ways of relating, quite without awareness, into the relationship with the therapist. For the therapist, it is meant to have an, 'as if' quality; you are meant to feel aware that you are being treated as though you are not yourself, as though you are some important historic figure in this individual's life. With Claire it didn't feel this way at all. It felt as though I was failing, and I had failed. That it was my failings as a psychotherapist that were on show. I had tried my hardest, done my best and it had not helped. That is where we found ourselves in our last session.

Then in the last ten minutes of her very last session she said could she change her mind and keep on coming to see me? That surprised me. There was a part of me that wanted to say 'no'. It felt as though she had won. She had reduced me to nothing in my own mind, and yet when she asked if she could keep coming I didn't reject her. I said she needed to make her mind up by the end of the session, but the decision was up to her, and I would support her, no matter what she chose to do. With three minutes remaining she said she had decided she would like to stay.

From that moment everything changed.

But I am going to pause here, because I had already learnt so much, even though I didn't realise it at the time. When I first thought about writing this series, I came up with a lot of different titles. They invariably included a powerful statement of rejection, along the lines of *Fuck off, I Don't Want to Eat, Go Away, I Hate You*, or *Why I Want to Stay Anorectic*. In the end I decided on the very simple *A is for Anorexia*. When you are anorectic it is your world.

So we end back with a massive and angrily expressed 'Do not Disturb Sign' on the door. But the thing is, if Claire and all those others really didn't want to be disturbed they could have slipped away, physically and emotionally and yet they chose not to. So if you open the door in the room on the cover, what happens? I would say a bomb goes off and by collecting and going through the fragments of the person, a new existence can be forged and things can be understood about the past.

So if you had an unexploded bomb inside of you, or indeed if you do, it is going to have an impact on how you behave. You are going to do everything to keep yourself safe, to stop it from going off. You are in your own mind protecting yourself and maybe others. Given that the unexploded bomb is a mess of feelings, memories, yearnings, desires and so much more; in fact, an inchoate mass then we can see the anorectic's self-starvation as a wise solution. It is a wall, to defend themselves against themselves.

They usually deny, with a certainty that makes little sense to those around them, that starving themselves is dangerous. It is a form of running away. We have already seen that hunger is addictive in itself and all addicts know that the substance distracts. Starvation is a time-consuming, mind-consuming, and body-consuming action that stops what has to be dealt with from being dealt with. Given that the core problem for an anorectic in her own mind is that she cannot make sense of anything inside of her it changes the scene of the action. She does not know that she can do anything about what is going on inside of her, but she does know she can control her appetite, with all of the attendant power and attention it gives her in relation to herself and others.

The agony for those who love an anorectic is that it leaves the problem with them, the observers to sort out and that is why there are two chapters on how to help. It is also what her body is screaming at you. I am not alright. Help, but don't.

Marilyn Lawrence in her book *The Anorexic Mind* comes to the same conclusion as Gianna Williams in terms of anorectics experiencing anything that is offered as an intrusive attack, but sees it being something the anorectic is born with. She starts off with a persecutory take on experience which makes navigating the world profoundly problematic.

The nature of the internal persecution

Janet Treasure argues that the anorectic 'minx', which is her name for the insistent demanding self-attacking voice of the anorectic, is not the woman speaking but her illness. My take on this is both 'yes' and 'no'. As we have discovered from looking at Ancel Keys work all of the men he starved became obsessed with food and their focus narrowed. However, how they responded psychologically was not uniform. Their fundamental aim was different too. They were there because they didn't want to fight, but they did want to help others. So, I would argue that some of what the anorectic woman feels is a response of her body to what she is doing to it, but that it is likely that this attacking part was quite alive and active before she became anorectic.

This is not unusual. Almost all the patients that I have ever seen, including many who have never had any issues with food, have had a highly developed super-ego that is causing them some trouble.

What is the super-ego?

It is a way of describing how one part of our mind works. In the thriving world of personal development which flourishes in the United States particularly it is referred to as negative self talk. In the UK it is often referred to as a negative voice in your head or having self-attacking thoughts. So by now you will probably know what I mean. It is the voice in your mind that tells you that you can't do things, that says you are no good, that knocks your achievements and tells you things like, you are stupid, fat, or ugly, just to name a few possibilities. You can probably add some more of your own here. It comes from unconscious guilt. Your mind is punishing you for having angry feelings and thoughts in response to some hurt that you have undergone and the link to this has gone as well. You have no real idea why you are in the prison you find yourself in, with no idea of who was the key, or how long the prison sentence is. The hurt can be an absence of something that was required, not necessarily the presence of something bad. So, for example, if we think about the young woman who had to hold her mother's hand whilst she had a bath. Let's say she found it very difficult, she felt frightened about her mother drowning, her own capacity to take care of her, and deep, deep down a quiet rumbling of her own needs calling from afar. They were not able to be responded to. Once again from far off comes the rumble of rage trying to make itself heard. This has to be stopped. She has to punish herself for this. She is not being good, loving her mother correctly, looking after her and so her super ego rushes to the fore and keeps her needs well out of reach and in their proper place, inaccessible to her.

The super-ego, ego and id were terms coined by Sigmund Freud at the beginning of the 20th century and were one of the ways he conceptualised how a mind works. I shall explain the other two parts a little later. But for now I want to concentrate on explaining the particular nature of the super-ego in the mind of an anorectic. There is no doubt that starving the super-ego is like feeding it rocket fuel.

The voice of an anorectic super-ego

Lynn Crilly quotes Eva who says she wishes she could have found a doctor who 'would have listened to me when I was more in control of my mind and before the horrible twisted voices took over completely'.

This is awful. I find it hard to even write at this point. The super-ego has a vicious voice that claims and takes over as much of the person as it can. It thinks and tells the woman that eating is bad, that she doesn't deserve to be alive, that being fat is a crime, that she is worthless, unlovable and never gets things right. It tells her everyone else is out to hurt her, to take away the one thing that makes her feel safe, her starving of herself. It punishes her brutally when she does eat. It tells her she is totally alone, that no-one can help, and that she is the holder of the truth, that she is different to everyone else. It says that the only hope lies in doing what she is doing. Everything outside of her is dangerous. There is no safety in the world except in her hunger and her pain. It punishes everyone who wants to help her. Her needs are to be unmeetable. It punishes her brutally if she tries to step outside of the anorectic prison. She will get hurt. It tells her, I told you so and see what happens when you try and leave. It can fill her with guilt at wanting to recover. It tells her that she is an extraordinary woman for being able to starve herself and show such strong self control and will power, as long as she keeps doing it. This is very hard work: to keep warm, to keep moving, to rarely get enough rest, but to keep on driving yourself. It is impossible to be inside the mind of an anorectic without remembering that much of their mind is preoccupied with dealing with their body. They force it on, deny its hunger, know its pain sometimes, and simply keep pushing on. Imagine the hardest physical challenge that you have undergone and do it every minute of every day. If you are anorectic it is meant to and does pretty much take up all of your available energy.

So this is what anyone seeking to help a woman who is suffering from anorexia is up against. It is very strong stuff. It is what Claire was communicating to me every way she could for a period of years. It is actually only a part of the mind, but in anorexia the rest is often silenced, but this does not mean it is not listening.

The underbelly of this and how to help shift it will be explained more in the chapter on the hard labour of recovery.

But, let's return to the two themes of sex and separation. So what I knew in a very visceral way was that it was only when I was really willing to let go of Claire and to give her the choice of staying or going despite having no idea how I might be equipped to help her that she let me in. She at that moment unlocked the door, both to herself and me.

What a good decision it was to have her stay. Our next move happened.

She had taken us both to the edge and this seemed crucial. Any act of separation means pulling away from another. It could be a therapist, a mother, a lover. The edge that Claire took me to was that of neediness. Her own need of me was too much to know and to bear. At that point all she could do was try to seek and not find, which meant that for session after session both of us felt desperate and unable to connect with the other person.

Opening the door on the cover of the book

So much of what an anorectic woman does is to defend against being known, because the fear is so great. Emma Wolf gives a poignant example in that she stopped allowing her family to touch her as she feared she would burst into tears. That sounds so potentially hopeful to me, but for Claire what I found inside her mind once the door on the cover had been opened was someone very small and very needy, who as an adult took an enormous risk in deciding to trust me to help her meet her needs, however incompletely.

I have always thought of the need to regress, as in some ways an emotional and physical attempt to start afresh, to get things sorted in a different and better way. There are great examples in the psychoanalytic literature, if you have time, money, love and confidence it can work. This is for people who are very troubled and in a variety of ways. There are two wonderful examples in the DVD Take These Broken Wings which you can find for free on the Wild Truth website.

Even the super-ego seems to go to sleep if the person is allowed to be small again, in some ways to start again. This was demonstrated very vividly in a chapter in Henri Rey's book *The Universals of Psychoanalysis*. He writes about a young anorectic woman he saw, Miss R, a psychology student from Durban, South Africa who when close to death had to be fed by a naso-gastric tube, which she liked.

She writes about growing a number of years in a number of months. 'I was a foetus, totally helpless, dependent, unaware of myself and of my feelings, in fact, so controlled that I never got round to ever showing what I truly felt or experienced in life'.

Ellen West wrote in one of her poems:

Creator, creator, Take me back!

Create me a second time And create me better.

In Todd Tucker's book on Ancel Keys work, I discovered a fascinating fact connected to one of the participants, Henry Scholberg, who scored highest of all on the 'psychotic' end of the Minnesota Multiphasic Personality Inventory. He was open about his own mental health difficulties. He had had awful nightmares at boarding school in India when he heard insane laughter around him and didn't know if it was in his head or out. Ancel Keys took him on, because references from those he had worked with were very good. He somehow survived the study, didn't cheat, didn't break down, and although he lost his temper as we have already heard, he felt awful about it. The interesting fact was that his scores at the end of the study moved from psychotic to neurotic. His physical regression through starvation seemed to help him emotionally and psychologically.

Claire expressed her wishes more simply: she wanted to be inside me like a baby, where the burden of responsibility could be handed over to me and where physically she could be safe and held. Her particular process of regression and how she moved back into life can be found in 'The Hard Labour of

Recovery'.

What is missing?

Just as the body of the anorectic becomes hard and her bones become brittle, so does her mind. She seems not to have any loving, kind, compassionate or softer feelings towards herself. These are what are missing.

The other thing that I thought was missing was how Claire felt about what I had written. I cut and pasted the parts of this book that included her and sent them to her. This was part of her reply: ' 'Firstly a detail that I remember differently? That session where I was going to leave but suddenly changed my mind... the way I remember it is that you told me that you would be moving to a new room and that this would be at your home... it literally felt like you were throwing me a life line... I was almost over the edge...'

I was thrown by her decision to stay being so much about the change of room. I had no idea that this was the case, or certainly no recollection of it, but it made sense as I thought more about it. Our first period of work took place in my home, the second consulting room was in a business block and the third was in my new home. The shock of being displaced and rejected was far greater for her than I realised at the time and fits with her need and ability to feel safe in the room we landed up in. The spaces we work with people in matter a lot too and can have a very powerful impact on them. Her anger was so powerful and present that I couldn't see the obvious. Separation was so hard for her, and I had thrown her out of my home and that was part of what was so intolerable.

Remember

If you are an anorectic you are more than your super-ego. You do not have to be so hard on yourself. If you love someone who has anorexia you now know what you are up against.

CHAPTER VIII

How to Help

This chapter is mainly for you if you are not anorectic. You may be a parent, a friend, a lover, a brother or sister, or someone who works with anorectics. You need to gain entry into the internal room of the anorectic and begin to help her know herself. The empty room on the cover, is like the empty body, the bones. It is a lie. Anorectics are full of feeling, so much so that they do not know what it is and they certainly cannot bear it. Whoever you are, knowing and remembering this fact will help. Also remember an anorectic herself is usually unable to look at what she has created and as we have seen in the last chapter is in the grip of her vicious super-ego. First here are some common goals for everyone who wants to help an anorectic. If you are anorectic you may want to speed on towards the end of the chapter where there are a couple of paragraphs addressing you directly.

Don't get caught up in eating talk

If you are starving, as Ancel Keys discovered you will

141

become more preoccupied with food.

As Emma Wolf said to her lovely boyfriend one morning, 'I can't eat now. I am too stressed from that orange.'

How anorectics decide on what and how they are going to eat is a very individual thing, full of its own impenetrable logic. Do not try and engage with it. Talking to an anorectic about what they eat, why they don't eat, how sensible it would be for them to eat more has the effect of adding fuel to the flames. Given their food systems have a life of their own they will simply find a convincing way of disagreeing with you, thereby strengthening their own resistance to change, which is obviously not what you want. If logic worked they would not be damaging themselves the way they are.

If you have the eating problem yourself, try and stop yourself from arguing with people about what you should and shouldn't eat and how you behave around mealtimes.

Remember touch is a powerful tool

Part of the deeply buried message that an anorectic body is telling you is keep away, and love me, I feel desperate. Given that the image in itself is so much more powerful than limited words, how we respond to the body in front of us is very important. When occasionally Claire and other anorectic women let me touch them, only the lightest of massage strokes felt possible to give to these fragile bodies.

But given the exile from a terrifying world that is outside the door of that unknowingly self-imposed prison, touch is like putting a hand through the wall. Or as one lovely woman used to say 'It's wonderful, but so painful'. Sometimes this brings a great sense of relief. Not always, as the defences may be so strong that they are not to be broached. But offering to gently stroke a back, rub her feet, give her a hug, although perhaps scary and hard to do will, I think, in some ways always help. It is painful because it can open the door to the knowledge of so much need.

Don't deny reality

This one is hard, but don't pretend everything is alright. Acknowledge her choice, but also acknowledge what it does to her, calmly and clearly. The aim is not to give the sufferer more feelings to hold, but rather for you to hold your own and let her know that you see her pain, isolation and suffering. You can recognise and acknowledge the pain of her position, even though she may not be able to acknowledge it herself.

Sometimes psycho-educational tools help

It can help to understand the physiological and psychological effects of starvation on the body. Reading about the Ancel Keys semi-starvation study might help. It shows the sufferer that they are not alone in what they are experiencing and that some of what is happening is happening to them is precisely because they are not eating.

Surprise can work. It can be a way of getting through impenetrable barriers. A bone scan showing an increasing weakness of the bones can sometimes work. It can shatter the fiction of omnipotence and invulnerability.

Find another way forward

Lynn Crilly writes about finding out about what her prospective patients like to do before she sees them so that she can help them grow in parts of their lives that they are able. This then can act like a virtuous circle and help the woman feel more inclined to tackle aspects of her anorexia. I am reminded here of Gina, who had severe obsessive rituals around eating, was very badly anorectic and had been for many years. She had always wanted to write a book and was very interested in essential oils. She sent off a book proposal to a publisher which was accepted and her book is now available on Amazon and in good book shops. She made one of her dreams come true. This was terrifying in many ways, but she stopped many of her obsessive rituals, which took up 5 to 6 hours a night and allowed herself to eat a wider variety of food without attacking herself for it. She stopped without having to force herself to. It simply happened as she engaged more with the health seeking parts of herself.

How and where to locate yourself psychologically

My own vulnerability and lack of expertise were I think crucial as to why Claire let me in. As a psychotherapist I feel this with every new person I meet to varying degrees. I try to make sure that I am joining them where they are, so that together, we can find a way of moving things forward. I am not doing something to them. An anorectic body and mind are not mine to mend. I can, with permission; help the sufferer become curious and compassionate towards herself. If you can achieve this position of consistent care and interest a great deal of the work is done, whether you are a psychotherapist, counsellor, friend or family member.

I now want to turn from some general to some specific points.

How to help an anorectic you live with

It is very simple; watching someone you love destroy themselves in front of you is pure torture. I don't think there is any other word for it, and my heart goes out to you. As Janet Treasure says about a parent having to help their child eat and how difficult it is: 'It takes the patience of a saint to do this day in, day out and meal after meal'.

Lena Zavarone, a child pop star who went on a crash diet at 13 and struggled with anorexia for 22 years died at the age of 35, when she contracted pneumonia. She had got married at

25. It lasted for only 18 months. Her husband, Peter Wiltshire, said later 'I had to go - it was self preservation. She was starving herself to death and there was nothing I could do' The agony of being a parent is that you can't abandon your child, regardless of how much you might want to, because you love them, not because you don't.

Janet Treasure's model is behavioural at the core and comes from the medical model where the view is that putting on weight is crucial to overcoming anorexia. This, in part comes from the work of Ancel Keys and colleagues in his research on starvation and re-feeding. So this is why so many of the early treatment models focused on re-feeding first, but it is very hard. There is also, of course the desire to keep the person who has anorexia alive.

So some of what your daughter or sister is feeling is due to what she is doing to herself. Although Janet Treasure says eating is non-negotiable and that has to be the baseline; it is a very tough one for the family. She is also very clear that for someone to recover from anorexia their feelings need to be felt and understood. She very usefully describes different ways people respond to having an anorectic in the house.

She uses animal metaphors. You might be a rhinoceros, a kangaroo, a jelly fish or a St Bernard. Few of us are saints and most will fall into being prominently more one animal than another, although at different times and with different levels of stress you may move from one to another.

A rhinoceros goes charging in, angry and probably fearful, determined to make the anorectic see sense. The charge usually occurs when the stress level in the house has become too much. When that tiny bit of salad is all your daughter eats, when everyone else is tucking in to roast chicken, roast potatoes and vegetables, which used to be her favourite. This is such an understandable thing to do, but your daughter will hate you for having got angry with her. She will feed attacked and profoundly misunderstood. So, if you can, desist. Somehow find a way to do something else with your rage at your impotence in the face of such distress.

A kangaroo seems a friendlier creature than a rhino and in some ways this is the problem. For according to Janet Treasure's schema a kangaroo, is like a kangaroo with a joey in its pouch. This means the parent, whether the mother, or father respond to the physical regression of the body of the anorectic, as though their daughter has become a baby, who needs to be treated like one. A fragile body does make people want to look after her, as does the carelessness with which an anorectic treats themselves. It can be very hard for a parent not to take over, to molly coddle their daughter. They may agree to all of her strange food requests, keep silent at certain times of the day when she wishes, protect her from other people, make sure she has a coat on when she goes out, fuss over her and treat her more like a three year old than the young adult she is. Try to resist doing this as much as you can. Think how you would be treating her if she was of normal weight and within reason try and treat her that way.

Don't let her rules rule you

This is one of the hardest tasks and links very strongly to kangarooing. It can lead to the daughter at home controlling all traffic in and out of the house, in fact controlling everything so that the whole family end up living in her anorectic prison. This is not going to help her move out of it. The problem is that when you are frightened that the person in front of you is going to die, you do become willing to do anything to try and help her survive. You may have to do this to keep yourself sane. But if you can, try not to. If you think about how you looked after her when she was two and a half or three, when she had tantrums in the supermarket, and got furious when she didn't get her way. That is what you have to trust. That she needs you to set boundaries so that she can rage and roar and keep rediscovering that you don't get destroyed by her anger and neither does she. In my book, every time an anorectic gets angry with me, it is not easy to be on the receiving end of, but it often leads to a breakthrough of one kind or another, so I am usually pleased.

I remember a fraction of a session with Nadia. I said something. I don't remember what it was, and she blew; from her core. She was so angry. I was frightened and concerned. Her anger gathered momentum. She said she hated me, asked me how could I say what I had said and walked out. It was not the end of the session. She bravely came back the following week, expecting me to reject her. I didn't, and we were able to do some good work together, which led to her making some significant changes in her life.

Back once again to Janet Treasure's invaluable metaphors. Next comes the poor old jelly fish. In reality jelly fish are poisonous and sting, but her jelly fish parent is the wobbly one. The one who cannot bear what she is seeing in front of her and collapses. Who wouldn't? It is hell. You might as well have your child stand there and say, 'look what you have created. I am a disaster, and I am your disaster'.

Be sad, be angry, feel guilty, bewildered and powerless if that is what you feel, and allow the pain in. Your daughter is giving you a chance to experience things that you probably don't want to. Paradoxically, the more you can tolerate and learn to survive these feelings, whatever they are, the better the environment for recovery you create for your child.

No parents or carers whatever their response should have to go through this alone. Ask for help. If you need support I offer a free monthly webinar for parents and friends of sufferers of eating disorders. You'll also find more information on-line and other resources in the following chapter. One of the best things you can do for your child is to show her that you can grow and change emotionally. Her illness may act as the catalyst, but your growth and capacity to tolerate the intolerable will model that change is survivable for her.

The ostrich does what ostriches do: buries his or her head in the sand. Once again, this is such an understandable response to impotence. For you fear there is so little that you can do, you stop trying and hope that magically the problem will go away. But sadly it doesn't. The emotional downside of this way of being is that it mirrors the anorectic's own unconscious defence of denial. It appears as though you think nothing is wrong and, of course, a lot is. As one parent in total denial of the problem said to his daughter, 'You eat like a little bird; I'm surprised you get by'.

The dolphin and the St Bernard are the top animal metaphors to go for. The dolphin gets the pace of push and pull, alongside or nudging the sufferer in just the right way and the St. Bernard is the perfect parent, calm, consistent, nurturing and loving. Don't forget these are also parts of who you are, the parent who is able to love her or his child without getting too entangled with them.

Feed your child if you can

Janet Treasure believes food is medicine and has to be taken everyday regardless of how difficult it is to do it. The aim is to get to the point where food is recognised as an essential fuel for the body and an important social activity. Remember, the brain requires seven times more calories than any other body part to function properly.

A re-feeding programme needs to be started. You do have to be careful. Re-feeding people who are starving with normal food too quickly can lead to their death, so you need to give your anorectic an invalid diet which is made up of soft food, or liquid food, a baby diet in many ways, and to start off at 1000 calories a day.

This is to be slowly increased, until a final goal of 2,000 to 2,500 calories per day is reached. The aim is to reach a BMI of 19.5 or above, when some of the impacts on the brain of starvation will begin to reverse. You need to eat an extra 500 calories a day to gain a pound or half a kilo in a week. One of Janet Treasure's books which she wrote with Gráinne Smith and Anna Crane is called *Skills-based Learning for Caring for a Loved One with an Eating Disorder: The New Maudsley Method*. It is full of useful information and good advice if you are up to going down this route. You need the patience, stamina and courage of a saint to do this; a St. Bernard perhaps?

There is much more in her books on this. Some families can do this and many cannot. Some anorectics do successfully find their own way to eating more as their emotional needs are understood, and can begin to be addressed.

How to help an anorectic who is a friend

The animal categories are likely to be useful for you to know about, so that you can begin to monitor your own feelings and really consider what a useful response to your friend might be. A number of anorectics I have worked with lost their friends, because they could not go on witnessing the self destruction they saw unfolding in front of them. This may be what you need to do. If you do, though, please tell Jane, or Claire or Peter, or whoever it is why you are pulling away and ask them if there is anything you can do to help them? If they say yes you can ask them to supper and say that you are going to ask them, and help them to eat something. You can negotiate together and ensure that you stay at the table for half an hour or so afterwards so that the food has a chance to get digested.

If you want to leave the tricky arena of food alone, then focus on pleasure. Find something you can do together that is fun. Acknowledge that the person is not just an anorectic. Do whatever floats your mutual boat. Ignore the anorexia at this point and remember the person inside. Be patient and be kind. They are having a very rough time inside there and remember that not eating is a destructive symptom, but it is not the main problem. The main problem is how your friend feels about herself and if you can really help her talk about this, it leads to change. Having fun together leads to an increase in trust and with that she may be willing to open up. If she does praise yourself and her too. You have brought a little hope into her anorectic prison. There is not a right or wrong, but if y o u can keep relating and loving the woman you know who has anorexia it can only help.

How to help an anorectic if you are a counsellor or psychotherapist

Hilde Bruch, my guide in so much to do with eating disorders, thought that anorectics did not have the ego strength to tolerate classical psychoanalytic technique. This means that as a psychotherapist you are not to not talk. This means do please talk. Reading Emma Wolf's description of her treatment at the Tavistock made me feel so sad. It is so unhelpful to create more persecution in a person who starts off terrified. Whether you have an opportunity to work long term or short term with an anorectic, key number one is to remember that as a result of starvation any natural levels of persecutory, competitive feelings have been ratcheted up by quite a few notches. You will, in fact, have someone quite paranoid coming into the room to see you. In essence, get on the anorectic's side, be with, not against, remain compassionate in the face of their cruelty, and begin to help her differentiate what is healthy from what is not, inside of her. You can find *Lost for Words: The Psychoanalysis of Anorexia and Bulimia* at Amazon and at www. abcofeatingdisorders.com you can download the chapter on 'Body Products and Transitional Phenomena' for free.

How to help yourself if you are anorectic

The very fact that you are reading this book fills me with hope. Somewhere inside yourself is a tiny part of you that knows something is not right. You may not know what you are trying to do by not eating and it may now be such a norm that is difficult to imagine doing anything else.

One of things that is so true of you is that you are a very strong willed, able person and the question is how you can turn this strength into an advantage for yourself.

If you are young and still live at home ask your parents for help.

Wherever you live find someone you can really talk to, who

is not a fellow anorectic. You have an incredible amount of talking to do. You may not know at this stage but it is true. There is so much inside of you that needs to come out, be sorted out and put back in.

Ask friends for help in any way you can.

Do your best to admit you have a serious problem that could eventually result in your death.

Your denial is a major stumbling block to your recovery.

Do not forget that you can recover. However much ground you have lost, however terrified you are, however hopeless you feel. Remember. There is a way out of your prison and back into life.

It is a route filled with very powerful feelings and difficulties,

but my goodness it is worth it.

In my mind eating and life are rather like asking which came first, the chicken or the egg. Start with one or the other and like a virtuous circle they will assist each other. The woman I mentioned who successfully got her book published still has major difficulties around eating, although she eats much more and with much less conflict than she used to. Claire has gone on to marry and have two children despite all of her terror around bodies and birth.

If you need help ask for it. There are lots of good resources out there. You can be helped with your terror. You can do it. There are many kinds of treatment which I detail below. Some address the anorexia directly, some less so. Remember, it appeared originally as a solution to difficulties you were having. Now it has become a difficulty in itself. Both of these things need to be tackled if you are to re-emerge into life. I offer a specialist service for a limited number of anorectic families every year

Remember if you are anorectic

Everyone who is born has a right to life, and that includes you. You can have a richer and more fulfilled one.

Remember if you are trying to help someone who has anorexia

You can help and remember to cherish who you have in front of you. Don't keep thinking about what might happen, relate to who you have with you, and do take care of yourself.

CHAPTER IX

The Hard Labour of Recovery

Physiologically, the aim for an anorectic woman is to reach a BMI between 19 and 25. The body will have periods then, if the person is ready for them emotionally.

As I have said before, it used to be thought that emotional and psychological work could only be done when weight had been put on. In my experience it is different depending on how thin the person is, and that if they want to they can engage and benefit from therapy at any weight.

I remember a lovely young woman I saw who, like Henri Rey's patient, seemed unconsciously to be aiming for collapse. She wanted to start again with her life, so, for her, she needed to begin again with her body. It was like playing with fire. I was terrified that she would collapse on the way to a session, or on the way out of one, or indeed in one. But our work consisted of us working out together that she wanted to go backwards, and for her, that felt like a way forward. In order to advance she needed to retreat, and she did. It seemed a strange kind of work which resulted in her admitting herself into hospital to be fed and taken care of. But, for her, it did mean the beginning of recovery.

Like Susie Orbach, I view most anorectics as being 'an embryonic self' deep down inside. This is problematic, as when they are very thin they are in an ego-syntonic state. This means quite simply that how they feel on the inside matches up with how they appear on the outside. So at some level they don't want to change things. Being anorectic suits them. That is why recovery is hard labour, because not only does the individual have to eat, but they have to begin to allow themselves to develop.

Some anorectics allow a little development in, just enough to stop them from being close to collapse physically and psychically. They remain profoundly preoccupied with food and hunger but are no longer at such risk of death. I see this group as living in a limbo land, a place where the terror of what is inside of them and what is outside can still be kept at bay. They remain on the nursery slopes of recovery and never make it to the hard labour.

In the Ancel Keys study, during the re-feeding phase, once the calories had been increased substantially, the men signed a petition demanding that the buddy system, whereby no-one was allowed to do anything alone, was abandoned. Josef Brozec, one of the researchers smiled as he told Keys if he didn't agree there would be a rebellion. 'Hungry people mindlessly follow orders; you feed them enough and right away they demand self-government'.

This is such a lovely way of describing what happens inside the mind of an anorectic. When the super-ego is in charge the woman follows the orders, not to eat, not to think, not to be and when she starts to eat there is room for something else to happen.

Of course, there is a massive difference between men who were part of an experiment whose intention was to help the starving in the world and women who choose to starve, full stop. For most of these women do not know there is someone inside them who has the capacity to self-govern, and that is what the hard work of recovering is about. They have to find a way of growing, and emerging into the world. Feeling as sensitive, as raw, as full of rage and sadness as a re-emerging woman does is difficult, for her and for those around her.

When the punitive super-ego is the boss recovery is impossible. Recovery is about recovering the other parts of the mind. These are the ego and the id. Miss R, Henri Rey's patient describes her emergence from her regressed place very well. She says about putting on weight, 'I just had to eat but there is no food or pills or any such aids to help one grow emotionally. To do that, I had to admit a lot of painful truths, a lot of concealed and crushed anger towards my parents, and, of course, the painful realization and eventual acceptance of my womanhood.'

What is the ego?

The ego as a concept was first named by Freud and was particularly taken up and worked with by his daughter Anna, and then by many other psychoanalysts and now is commonly used to mean someone who thinks almost too well of themselves. In fact, I like to think of it as the healthy part of a person that is able to relate both to him or herself and to others. It has a capacity to grow and can take in nourishment and digest it, whether physical or emotional. This baby moves from being embryonic to, as Colwyn Travarthen, Emeritus Professor of Child Psychology and Psychobiology at Edinburgh University, said, 'a passionate communicator'. This is the baby that emerges once the anorectic shell is cracked. What she needs at this moment is someone who understands the hell and the passion of being reborn fully grown and years behind. And as

Freud said, 'The ego is first and foremost a bodily ego'.

What is the id?

The id is the powerhouse, the engine that fuels everything else. It is a mess of every feeling and experience you have ever had in your whole life. It is the source of health, because by beginning to know yourself and what you feel life can become easier. This may sound trite, clichéd and easy. It is not. It is complex and very challenging work.

So the hard labour of recovery starts with a woman beginning to turn her gaze with curiosity and compassion, towards herself. It starts with a location. The problem lies not outside of herself and outside of that door on the cover, but inside the room. She is the author of her own distress and her eyes need to be turned towards herself.

She views herself as being as grey and barren as the room itself. She will tell you that she is empty, but this is simply a false floor. She is full, too full, so full of feelings that she can never attend to because the super-ego is in charge, battering her so comprehensively. She hurts herself because she doesn't know she is hurting. It is reminiscent of that old adage that 'attack is the best form of defence'. She at the same time experiences everyone making demands of her, which is why the door is shut. She feels she has no space. She defends against what lies outside of her. Every contact feels persecutory. If you are always under attack you have no time or space for yourself and remain hyper-vigilant to what is going on around you, for your very survival is threatened. There is danger outside and there is the terror of what is inside.

It reminds of me of Elizabeth, who had been abused as a child and attributed it all to herself: 'Either I am so unattractive that no one will look at me or I am so dangerous sexually that I devour men'. No wonder she was frightened. Appetite is scary.

So the process of recovery starts. It is extraordinary how anorectics don't know how to talk about themselves at all, except for their anorexia. It is as if they have had no life, no history, no experiences to process. Anorexia and keeping everything out of their awareness is their life.

When Claire decided to stay and work with me, she began to talk. These are the kinds of things that filled the sessions. She began to talk about herself. In the section on the body I have written about how she began to try to work out what a female body did, how it worked, what it could and couldn't do. She became less frightened of herself.

Another aspect of this was her on-going curiosity about my

body. As the scene of the action and the preoccupation is so often with the people who surround an anorectic rather than herself, this was a creative half-way house. She did talk about what was in her mind, and that was a preoccupation with my body. She wondered what it was like for me to be a woman. She had dreams about me reaching up for a book on a high shelf. That consulting room had books shelves up as high as the ceiling. She imagined looking up my skirt. She wanted to know more about how a woman's body worked, indeed, how mine did. This didn't feel sexual, but curious.

She began to allow herself to know how needy she was. How desperate, how small and how young and defenceless she felt a great deal of the time. She moved from wanting to look up my skirt to being back in the womb. My womb of a room would do. She had gone from rage to exposing vulnerability which took a great deal of courage and bravery for her to do. She was finding her own way of starting again.

She viewed herself as insatiable and monstrous in appetite. She had concretely locked the door, so no-one could get in and she couldn't get out. By shrinking herself she had tried to shrink her problems.

It is hard to convey how delicate this work felt at this stage.

It felt like the work of life and death. If you are a parent and remember having your first child, this is as close to bringing the feeling in the room alive for you. Imagine the risk for an adult, a troubled, hyper-sensitive, mixed up woman choosing to allow herself to feel like an infant. This is what Claire did. She tested me and threw everything at me to see if I was sturdy enough, and when she found that I was, she could let go.

In the letting go everything became different. The very air in the room seemed to change. At times I became acutely aware of my breathing, of my body, of every move and sound I made. Everything had an impact-on her as well as on me. She didn't want to leave the sessions. She wanted to stay. If not in the room with me, she imagined finding a cupboard under the stairs and living there. She did not want to go back out into the outside world. The pain of it felt too much, and yet she bravely endured and moved onwards. Session after session. Often, a few minutes before the end of sessions, she would get angry and rejecting, her tone became more tense, her voice louder, as though it was tremendously hard for her to go. She had to gear herself up to leave. Once, at the door of the room I remember her turning and saying to me, 'It's like having my breath cut off'. Her life hung in the balance every time she left. What courage it took for her to come back session after session. This is where the going over and over something to manage it began to work. She did live, and so did I, despite the feeling that she was going to die as she left the room. This is, in my mind, what working with regression means, that going back, in order to start coming forward. Claire chose the emotional rather than the concrete path of tube feeding and hospitalization. This led to her deciding to eat more herself.

It takes such courage to start again. Although understanding why someone becomes anorectic is complicated its impact on the body and mind is not. If you are anorectic you are stopping the clock of your own emotional development. You may keep going through the motions, but the things that really need attention inside of you are not being attended to. Susie Orbach thinks in terms of arrested development. It is even worse, as though their arrested development has been arrested. As Hilde Bruch puts it: 'They lack awareness of their own resources and don't rely on their feelings, thoughts and bodily sensations'. This leads to them feeling so without resources, which actually they are not. As Karol, one of Hilde Bruch's patients said, 'I am like the frosting on the cake with no cake inside'.

The agony of recovery and why it is such hard work is that you feel out of sync with others. Catching up is hard, and there is a lot of pain to be felt. The realisation of what you have missed, what you have not had or been able to work out, is enormous, and it takes time to trust that another person can actually bear you and help you.

Someone with anorexia feels other, feels like a freak, but, as we now know, it is likely that she felt that way inside long before she became anorectic. There is no doubt that anorexia can exacerbate the feeling of difference and of being odd.

So the id and ego dance in the room together. Thought and words become more possible as the feelings are felt and the terror diminishes. The ego becomes stronger and begins to look outwards. Claire moved out from living with her mother to living in a house run along psychotherapeutic lines. It was a shared house, where group therapists came twice a week to run house meetings. She continued having therapy with me too.

My process in many ways mirrored hers. Step one was the staying with and attending to our breathing, allowing her to slowly grow and take up more space. My job was to digest her feelings of terror and her need. It got to the point where I was able to say I felt like I was walking on eggshells. The timing was good, and the next step came. That feeling of having a new baby in the room changed, and her very presence felt more substantial.

Her own curiosity got engaged. I remember her asking me what she looked like one day. I remember saying she seemed lanky and a bit uncoordinated, as though she didn't quite know how she fitted together. I now have the image of a foal taking its first steps. She smiled. She could hear this and take it in. Later I remember saying to her that she seemed bigger and that I wasn't talking to her about her weight. She seemed to be allowing herself to take up more space in the room. She seemed to have arrived in herself.

I hope I have given you a sense of the intensity, the challenge and the joy it was working with Claire. When I showed her what I had written about her she wrote back 'I was quite shocked at how much I had hurt you... I had no idea... I guess that's the point in a way?! It was also quite painful to look back at myself and that time in my life, which seems so far away now... and obviously, a big THANK YOU from me'.

Shock

When the super-ego is in charge there is no room for self-compassion or curiosity. There is self-obsession but not self-knowledge. Recovery is so hard because to move forward you need to know where you have come from and what you have done to yourself. This is shocking, particularly when someone comes face to face with the denial of the consequences of self starvation-which means they might have killed themselves without intending to. That they have hurt themselves, sometimes permanently, is hard to bear.

Compassion towards your own body is important. It is here. It needs attention. One woman found that rubbing her feet with her hands gave her comfort. She was being kind to herself. This is a new world she is entering, and, as she does so, her relationship with her eating is likely to change.

Eating

When you have been eating very little and you try to eat more it hurts, physically, emotionally and every which way. Claire used to say 'it was like my insides were being ripped to shreds'. Emma Wolf talks of the agony of every bite. I'm aware that Claire's story contains little about her direct problems with food, apart from this quote. Unlike Janet Treasure, my own way of working leaves the eating in the anorectic's hands rather than my own. It sometimes comes in briefly, normally when help, support and understanding are needed about how hard having food in the stomach is.

This is where understanding your own super-ego is so

important. You need to differentiate the healthy or helpful thoughts in your mind from the ones that are not. So 'I don't deserve to eat' or 'This will make me fat' are unhelpful, untrue and cruel thoughts to have towards yourself.

This is an incredibly hard battleground. Use whatever weapons and tools you can to help yourself. I remember one psychotherapeutic community which used to have a number of anorectic patients. They used to leave nuts, raisins and delicious morsels around the place so that things could be eaten without being noticed.

The son of a friend of mine stopped eating as an adolescent. Not entirely. He only ate brie and chocolate. She asked what she should do. I said make sure there is a lot of brie and chocolate around. She did, and he found his own way forward.

Often anorectics not only eat very little, but their diet is often limited to two or three kinds of food. Part of the hard labour of recovery is risking eating some of the things on the 'how on earth did I ever to manage to eat' list that most anorectics have. It might have been baked potatoes, toast, Mars Bars or carrots. It is often a real breakthrough when something can be added or changed, even if the calories remain the same to start with.

Ancel Keys was shocked at how hard it was for the men

to regain weight, particularly those in the group who had been given the lowest amount of calories. In fact weight loss continued, usually as oedema stopped. Still, after six weeks, the men who had been given an additional 400 calories per day had only put on a tenth of a pound. Even those receiving the highest calorific intake, of over 3000 calories per day, had only gained 6.5lbs after six weeks. This so surprised Keys that he changed his plan and gave an additional 800 calories day to everyone. It was still really hard for the men to gain weight. Even by the end of the re-feeding phase no one was up to where they started from. Claire found it hard to believe how much she could eat before it made any difference to her size. She had to work hard to gain weight.

A few of the men who dropped out displayed binge eating behaviour, and sometimes anorexia does seem to be a defence against bulimia, and when this defence breaks down it is a good sign, although if you have anorexia you are unlikely to think so.

So regaining weight is really hard work. You have to eat an awful lot to put on weight.

Ignoring the super-ego: that cruel internal voice

One of the problems when someone starts to eat more is that the super-ego gets very agitated and talkative. Arguing with a super-ego doesn't work. It is rather like trying to persuade a lion who is about to pounce that it is not a good plan. So sticking with the lion analogy what else might work? Well, running away is good. Having a gun and using it would work. Or, if it is purely an imaginary lion, ignoring it and doing something else might do the trick.

All of these things involve action. And one of the most noticeable attributes of an anorectic is that she allows herself to be eaten by the lion and then feels unable to do anything about it.

So Lynn Crilly helps women ignore their super-egos and turn to what they enjoy. She helps them move from passive to active. *Take These Broken Wings* shows talking cures that worked with two schizophrenic patients. One of its stars is Joanne Greenberg who wrote about her own therapy in the classic book *I Never Promised You a Rose Garden*. She speaks about the pain of her madness and how she made it out into the world and then things came crashing down again, and she found herself back in hospital. Then she tells of the time she was on a bus in 1958, and the voices started again, and she thought, 'Wait a minute, Hon... What's this all about? Oh, mother's little sweetheart. Let's figure this out'. She responded to the voices in her mind. The interviewer asked her if it was unusual for her to ask herself about what was going on, and she said schizophrenics never did that. It was the first time in her life that she took an active position in relation to her own mind and the messages it was giving her. And she said to herself 'Suffer a little smarter' The segment ended with her smiling and slightly rolling her eyes and saying 'Me and my minds'.

My aim in quoting the above is to show the massive internal power we all have when we take an active and positive position in relation to ourselves.

Anorectics are not alone in this. Many people who come to therapy have super-egos that have run away with them, and it takes hard work to stop, see, separate and take action.

So the question becomes, how do you move from passive to active? Sometimes the steady drip of care and attention allows a modelling which can be mirrored. Claire moved from hating and distrusting everything about herself and me to slowly valuing the space I provided, the feelings she had, and the thoughts we shared. This led to her taking in a way of treating herself that was kinder and more respectful of herself. Unsurprisingly, this meant she also was able to be more appreciative and kinder to me.

When the super-ego is in charge the ego loses its voice and

it needs to find it. This means moving into new territory. You have to leap. You just have to do it if you want to get better. Internally you are creating something new, and you have to keep pushing and pushing until something different comes into your mind. Here is an example. Emily found the task of staying alive highly problematic. Her super-ego kept on misinforming her that everyone would be better off without her. That she took up too much space, and caused them too much worry. Her first task was to identify that it was misinformation. It was in effect an internal liar, someone who was not on the side of her life, her capacity to love, her hope and her health. So I asked her what she was going to do about it. This is a good question to ask yourself, and keep ploughing on past the 'I don't knows'. She paused and then a tiny smile crossed her face. I asked what had come into her mind. She said 'I'm going to lock her in the attic'. What a great and creative response. She had imaginatively turned her super-ego into a person she could lock away. This meant she would not have to listen to her super-ego's voice. I said 'and then?' and then she was able to speak about herself as someone who wanted to live, who had just been let down by a man. She allowed herself to feel both the angry and sad feelings she had about this experience, rather than staying caught in the grip of her agitated super-ego.

What gets forgotten is that you can step in and take action, but you may need help in order to do so. Miss R, gives a lovely example of talking back to her super-ego when it starts telling her yet again that she needs to have a body she is happy with; she says to herself , 'Just one final warning, woman, woman, your mind is still distorted that's all I have to say'.

Mourning

As Julian Barnes says in his book *Levels of Life*, 'One grief throws no light upon another,' and there are so many varieties of grief. And yet there are common stages and identifications that do occur. Shock is the first. The line between life and death is mind-blowing, for always and forever. As a young person it is even harder to process, and the body, once again, seems to run away with itself unless a person can be helped to mourn. And a major part of what has to be mourned is the life they have lived so far.

Mourning sucks. It goes on and on. There is such sadness that comes in waves, sometimes expected and sometimes not. What you are likely to find with an anorectic, if someone they love has died, or someone has left them for whatever reason, is that this process of grieving is unlikely to have taken place. They did not have the chance to be sad in whatever way they needed to be.

Recovery is hard labour, and it hurts. I think it hurts more than having the feelings in the first place. This maybe fanciful - I'm not quite sure about it - but I think it maybe like when a part of your body goes to sleep and it is very painful when it comes back to life. As Miss R put it when she had put on weight and became bigger, 'I almost feel like a 'grown-up', new, fresh and tender, so much so that I am still a foetus or a very young infant in this new role.'

Part of the pain is the agony of knowing that you are capable of doing something different. It is impossible not to feel real sadness for what you have done to yourself. You have to mourn for the self you have not been for the years that you have not been her. But if you are feeling sad, it already means you are moving forward. As we have seen, envy, that simply horrible destructive, feeling may have had a role in instigating the anorexia. The super-ego in some ways gives voice to envy, and one thing to watch out for as you move back into the world is that the super-ego will try and strengthen itself in the face of your progress. It will in effect try and stop you in your tracks again, and so once more you need to stop, notice and take action so that you can allow your own best efforts to continue.

An anorectic body will also need to grieve for her anorectic self. It kept her separate, safe and special. The pain of being ordinary is hard. Different ways need to be found to comfort and nourish the self and to interact with the world around you. You have to deal with the dilemma of wanting and not wanting help in a more ordinary way. The body can no longer do the talking. The woman has to use her mouth and words to express how she feels, what she thinks and what she wants. She has to let food in and let her own communication out in words.

What I don't know how to do is to communicate to you how painful this is. 'Feelings', as a word, often sound clichéd and trite. But we are talking here about agonising pain. Perhaps imagine the pain that mummified body in the British Museum would have if she came back to life. It is that kind of intensity that is going to have to be gone through before life becomes easier to live.

I asked Elizabeth what she would have needed to have happened for her not to become anorectic, and she said, 'I would have to have been seen and heard'.

Remember

Life is worth living. If you can, do start saying 'yes', not 'no'.

CHAPTER X

How to Create Your Own Successful Care Package

This chapter is written for you if you have anorexia and want to do something about it. This is another of those moments when life can change. Often patients who begin to talk about something that is very important in the last few minutes of the session will say to me, 'How much time do I have left?' and I might answer 'Seven minutes'. They will then say, 'There's no point telling you about it then'. I say 'Yes, there is. It is amazing how much you can do in seven minutes'. And then we do it.

Taking the plunge, whenever, and for however long is the hardest thing to do. As a sufferer one of the missing planks in your life is likely to be hope and by reading this, some of it is beginning to sneak in. A woman, of whom I am very fond, who I have worked with for a long time, told me that when she broke down at university and was terrified of going mad, she saw her GP who said to her 'Someone, somewhere will be able help you,' and if you are reading this I believe this is true for you, too.

The question is then how do you find that person. The answer is by trial and error. Despite the desire for perfection and getting things just right, the road to recovery is not only hard labour but often uneven and patchy.

So to begin, think of one thing that would help. One small thing. Anything, and then put it into practice. One woman I know had a shower in her home and wanted to be able to have a bath, where she could lie down and be held by the bath and the warm water. She sorted it.

You may decide to increase the amount you eat, or not. Or you may decide to add a different kind of food which has the same calorific value but that you may not have eaten for years.

We have looked in the previous chapters, both implicitly and explicitly, at how important kindness is. Treat yourself as though you matter, as though you are someone of value, even if you don't feel it. Research shows that you have to say a positive thing roughly ten times to every negative thought for it to begin to stick. Change from calories to how many kind things you can say to yourself. So the sooner you are able to push some of those negative thoughts out the better.

Once you have decided you are going to in some way help and be kind to yourself, you are already on your way to recovery, so what next?

Dealing with your super-ego

You are starving and hurting yourself by choice minute after minute, day after day. If someone you loved was doing this to themselves, what would you say? Try and say it to yourself. The first step is to stop it and the second step is to begin to introduce kindness, self-care and compassion into how you treat yourself. You have to be creative here. You are likely to come up with a big blank when thinking about yourself, so think of an injured friend, lover, animal, whatever works for you and how you would speak to him or her to comfort, reassure and support them. These are the kinds of phrases that you need to say to yourself. I shall just give you a few examples to get the ball rolling. 'It'll be all right', 'I'm here with you', 'You are doing so well', 'I know you are in pain, but you can bear it and get through this' and 'You are really brave, stay with me, you can make it'. Use them to help you get through each minute of every day. Be kind. You can do it.

When you start doing this it will provoke the super-ego even more. You may feel mocking, critical, stupid about speaking to yourself in a kinder way. This is just the next level of self-attack. Ignore it and keep being kind, as being cruel to yourself is never helpful.

Covering different bases

All of us have different areas that need attending to, our bodies, our minds and our hearts and our souls, depending on whether you are a believer or not. Let's now look in more detail at the external resources which are available to you.

So if you decide you want to seek outside help and you are a sufferer how do you go about it?

You first need to think very clearly about what kind of help is going to suit you. This is not about what works for someone else.

Part of what has happened in your mind is that you have lost touch with how central your thoughts, feelings, and body are to your own life. The programme you want to construct for yourself is one that is going to take all of these aspects of you into consideration and help you move into the future.

There are so many different forms of help and therapy available. They vary enormously, depending on what country you live in and whether you are an urban or rural dweller. There is a massive difference in provision in the United Kingdom depending on where you are. The same I imagine will be true for you wherever you live. What most of us do have access to is the internet. This can be a great place to start, but if you are beginning to be pro yourself, any 'pro ana' sites are not for you. If you don't know, these are sites that encourage people to starve themselves. They are illegal because they are no good if you are interested in living and loving rather than hating and dying. If you find any do report them to Google and they will take them down. There are really good resources on line.

Online resources

The choice is endless, from support groups, to such organisations as BEAT, standing for Beat Eating Disorders, Anorexia and Bulimia Care and the Succeed Foundation in the UK and the National Eating Disorders Association in the United States. If you want nutritional advice you can find it. If you want therapy on Skype you can find it. But again, what you need to do, is find a way forward that works for you. There is increasing political interest in tackling low self-esteem and body image difficulties in young girls, and the Be Real Campaign is excellent. Their website is full of useful information and facts and figures and part of their mission statement reads

'Be Real is campaigning to change attitudes to women's bodies and helping all of us put health above appearance and being confident in our bodies'.

Books to read

Again there is a long list. Some of my favourites re treatment are by Janet Treasure, just pop her name in Google and a variety will come up. If it is about understanding and recognising what has happened to you, I would read Hilde Bruch, whether it is her book *Eating Disorders: Obesity, Anorexia Nervosa, and the Person Within, The Golden Cage* or *Conversations with Anorexics.* Another classic writer in the field is Susie Orbach, whether you read her original *Fat is a Feminist Issue* or her more recent *Hunger Strike.* There are memoirs written by recovered or recovering anorectics such as Marya Hornbacher's *Wasted: A Memoir of Anorexia and Bulimia* or Emma Wolf 's *An Apple a Day.* They both show the richness and the horror of being anorectic and how hard it is to recover.

How you decide who is best for you, if you want to have an actual person involved, requires careful thought.

Different kinds of treatment

Do you come from the kind of family where things have

not been talked about very much, but where with some help perhaps they can be? Family therapy can be very helpful if you are in the age range of 18 to 25 and have not had the illness for too many years. It is scary and can be very difficult, but it is worth looking into if you are brave.

Medical treatment

As with psychological treatment, this is rather a lucky or rather unlucky dip in the UK and probably in other parts of the world too. Some doctors are very well informed about eating disorders, and some are not. You might find an empathic doctor who is able and willing to listen and be with you, or you might find someone who says unhelpful things, like, 'It would be a good idea if you ate more'. If you do find a good doctor, that you like, even if they don't know a great deal about it, you can help them help you. You could ask to be weighed regularly if that helps, you could ask to be referred to a specialist eating disorder unit, and a nutritionist and a psychotherapist. You could ask to be tested to see if you have osteoporosis or are on the way to it. Depending on the severity of your anorexia you may want your heart and blood pressure to be checked as well.

In some countries there is the option of residential treatment.

As I briefly mentioned earlier there is sometimes a link made between eating disorders and addictions and some of the big addiction centres do treat anorexia as well. Again a moment with Google and you will find them.

Talking treatments.

This means psychotherapy or counselling. Be really fussy about this. There are a lot of really excellent, courageous and able counsellors and therapists out there and there are some duds too. You will know pretty quickly whether someone will suit you, and that is all you are after. What is really difficult is trusting yourself to gauge whether someone is ok. Test them and find out. It is much better to move if you haven't felt helped by someone than to stay. If you get through ten in quick succession, that in itself is worthy of thought and reflection. There is never going to be someone who will understand you completely, never make a mistake and always get it right. That is not what you need to look for. As I suggest above you need to find someone who can help and I bet there is someone out there who can. Once you have found someone, ask them to help you find others, to give you, the practical, psychological and physical support that you need.

One of the big decisions you need to make is whether you want to have treatment in a group or individually. In my experience when you are anorectic you are profoundly short of the kind of attention you need and that would lead me, if I were you, to go towards individual therapy first. Later, when you feel stronger, more lithe emotionally and intellectually a group might be brilliant, but not at first.

There are a bewildering number of psychotherapeutic models available. Again, treat yourself as though you matter. If you want to see someone more than once in a week you need to find a psychoanalytically informed psychotherapist. If once a week seems like it will be enough or less then you have many other options. You can go for the more thought based ones, such as CBT (Cognitive Behavioural Therapy) or NLP (Neuro Linguistic Programming), the more body based energy and trauma models such as EMDR (Eye Movement Desensitization and Reprocessing) or EFT (Emotional Freedom Techniques), or the combined but more difficult ones such as ISTDP (Intensive Short Term Dynamic Psychotherapy).

Primarily non-verbal treatments. Massage

When I set up my Centre for Eating Disorders in 1989 I used massage as a major part of the treatment. I believed and still do that for anorectics and some others who suffer from real difficulties with their bodies, massage can calm them down.

If, as we know, even though it may only be on the edge of your consciousness that terror is one of the key issues around anorexia, then one of the first things I would want you to be able to do for yourself is to help yourself feel safer. A good massage therapist can do this. It needs to be someone you see regularly, someone you like and someone who has a good pair of hands. You need to be able to lean on them. If you can do this, you are on your way to recovery. Once again, be brave, and get a recommendation from a friend. If that works, great, if not, remember to always find someone YOU like. This is a real gift that you can give yourself.

Equine interventions

One of my favourite primarily non-verbal interactions is with horses. There are two main strands within the equine world, one is equine assisted learning and the other is equine assisted psychotherapy. Whole books are written on these matters, and, in fact, I would like to write a book about it, but for now I am sticking to the essentials. The first is often aimed at companies and individuals who are having difficulties deciding which direction to take in their lives. There is one cross-over model I know of which is the Horse Course, a Charity set up and run by Harriet Laurie. She has adapted natural horsemanship principles into a week-long behavioural course which she runs for prisoners, and increasingly for other groups, including mental health patients. She has created her own model which helps participants move from stuck to unstuck. It is very action oriented, and there is no expectation that you will talk about your difficulties. It is all about watching, learning, trying and doing. It works, you learn a lot and it is good fun. She trains people all over the United Kingdom. You can find more about her work at www.thehorsecourse.org. You are not expected to know anything about horses. It involves working with them from the ground, rather than riding them.

Equine Assisted Therapy comes out of years of man-to-horse interaction and love. People have long asked why is it that horses are so good at helping humans, and why is it that humans feel so helped by horses? Part of my answer is that it is mysterious, and we don't really know, but there a couple of differences in our brains which researchers believe helps to explain a little of it. The brain of a horse is made up largely of the feeling part with a very small part that does the thinking. In humans the balance is pretty much the other way around. What this suggests is that horses that pick up on the slightest emotional shift in their leader, and respond instantly to it, are in fact very good at knowing how to regulate emotion. They can help humans regulate their own emotions at quite an unconscious level.

Of course they are also great to touch and we know from research with dogs that stroking helps the person who does the stroking, and hopefully it is pleasurable for the cat, dog or horse as well. Many anorectics have effectively banished touch, as it leads to the too dangerous place of vulnerability and feeling. But standing next to a horse and choosing to put your hand on their neck is a different matter. I spent a great day observing some of Harriet's work in a prison and was very moved when, during the breaks, some of the young men would, rather surreptitiously, stroke the horse they were holding whilst it was grazing. You could see the nourishment and the softening that took place. There is a whole model similar to individual therapy that can work with horses. I love having a horse or two helping the people I work with, and I offer it as part of my specialist anorectic service.

In order not to get too carried away I shall just give one example. It is one of those ridiculous true stories that I still don't know how to make sense of. Ruby was 11 when a friend contacted me and asked me if I thought I could help Ruby.

She had anorexia, and her mother was at her wits end. I said I didn't work with people who were so young and suggested a few other options. Slightly to my surprise I found myself saying that if she wanted to bring Ruby to play with the horse for a day, no fee, no therapy, just experimenting, she would be welcome.

I felt anxious, but thought that a day in the countryside, away from her normal life would be a good thing for Ruby. I worked out a tentative plan of action. It did not involve asking Ruby any questions about herself, but rather asking her to make decisions on her own behalf. She had to choose which horse to work with. She had to learn how to safely move around the horse she chose, and she had to learn how to use some tools, such as a stick with a rope on, a halter and a lead rope. There were also the options of grooming a horse, and perhaps sitting on one for a little while. I said to her that horses were good at picking up on feelings and I got her to stand in an empty paddock with horses either side and asked her to whack the ground with the long string attached to the stick. It is like a whip but with rope where the lash would be. She did. Some of the calmer horses got a bit worried and moved away smartly. A couple of them were really disturbed, until she kept going, and they got used it. I had some apples. I had one myself, offered one to the horse and one to her. They all accepted. She then chose to play with a super-responsive and sensitive horse.

The game was simple. The horse was grazing and Ruby wanted it to come with her. I said to get it to do so she needed to really focus on where she wanted to go, emotionally and with her eyes and then begin to consciously bring her energy up. She was not to pull on the rope. It was to lie over her hand. I saw her look up, I saw her energy come up. The horse raised her head and they moved forward together, as one. Ruby ate her lunch. She was a very thin stick. She has been eating ever since.

Music, art and movement therapies

These are often on offer as part of the in and out-patient treatment and can be very helpful.

Nutritional advice

If you think some nutritional advice will help, find some. It is more an art than a science, but again if you can find someone you trust who can help you with your eating habits in any way then go for it.

In-patient treatment

My knowledge of resources outside of the UK is very limited, so you may want to skip this section, unless you live in the UK. Here, there are a variety of private and NHS solutions. Your route to NHS treatment is through your GP who can then refer you to a specialist eating disorder unit. If you have money you can usually self refer either to some of the private hospitals that offer in-patient treatment for anorexia, such as the Priory Group or the Nightingale Hospital. Some of the private addiction clinics also offer in-patient support. Once again, if you are doing this for yourself, then visit a few places, get a feel for what will suit you best before you finally decide.

Specialist bespoke multi-modal solutions

Many of the hospitals including Ellern Mede Ridgeway which works with young anorectics up to the age of 18, offer programmes with a variety of activities and ways of helping, including some of the non-verbal methods suggested above.

My own eating disorder service works by trying to discover what and how change can take place for the individual sufferer and for the family. The programme is aimed at adolescent and adult anorectics. Family might be parents, partners, siblings, children, or any combination thereof. The aim is to do a very thorough assessment so that on-going work can be targeted to produce good results. To this end I have a team of colleagues who help with various aspects of the process I am going to describe below.

It works like this. The first step is for the person with anorexia to be seen by me alone for two three hour sessions. In order to make sure that the ground is beginning to shift and to sustain momentum the gap between sessions is to be no more than two weeks. The next step would be to see the whole family together. This would take place, not in a consulting room, but in a covered arena or a field working with horses on the ground, but not riding them. This would take a whole day. And, lastly, there would be two family sessions which would take place in a consulting room in London. These family sessions would last for an hour and a half each. After the first one, specific plans will be suggested for everyone. These may include different kinds of physical, psychological and or nutritional interventions. At the end of the second session progress and obstacles are to be assessed. From here on the way is up. Follow up family sessions would then take place every few months depending on what is needed. I take on a limited number of families each year. Go to www.abcofeatingdisorders.com to find out more.

Extreme solutions.

Lena Zavarone had anorexia from age 13. In her 30s she found her depression to be intolerable and asked to have brain surgery to help with it. She had said to the surgeon that she would kill herself if he didn't perform it for her. It did seem to work, and she started being interested in the staff around her and began to look people in the eye. Her weight was still only around 5 stone. She sadly developed a chest infection which turned into pneumonia, and she died at the age of 35.

Your own extreme solution maybe deciding to leave home, getting a job, to start dating, whatever it is, if it is taking you towards leading your life, then take it.

Remember

There are lots of options. Help is out there and you can have a more fulfilling life.

CHAPTER XI

Conclusion and What Next?

So, we get to the end of *A is for Anorexia*. Anorexia is, as I hope this book has informed you, a hell of an illness to have. Recovering from it is possible, and if you are someone who has done so, or have helped someone to then you are a remarkable person. As Janet Treasure said about helping starving family members to eat, 'It takes a saint'. In the real world there are no saints, but only desperate, determined and stubborn people.

As I finish this book I realise what a big project I have undertaken. In the world of the internet publishing an information book is meant to be a simple thing to write. You just find out the information on a subject and write it down. That sounds so easy. What that prescription doesn't tell you is how hard it is to do this if you know quite a lot about it already.

My knowledge of anorectics, their bodies and their minds is very specific. I have not worked in an eating disorder unit nor been involved directly in re-feeding programmes. Others have much more direct and relevant experience of these two things. I am not a medical doctor or a nutritionist. What I do know something about is the pain of parents with children who have anorexia, and the courage that someone has to have to turn up in my consulting room, either for themselves or a member of their family.

The anorectics I have been privileged to know sometimes find me when they can't get help elsewhere. This may make them a particular group.

My aim has been ambitious. I wanted to help you understand anorexia from the outside in and from the inside out. Hopefully, I have shown you how long it has been around, what people have thought about it, the facts and figures connected to it, what it is an attempted solution to, what goes on inside the mind and body of an anorectic and how anorexia can be overcome.

Whenever I finish writing an article or a book I often find that I want to start all over again. There is so much more to go into here. I realise that there are three very specific areas that I do write about here, but where there is room for much more work to be done. The three areas are: how to help get out of an anorectic mindset, how to work with anorectics if you are a therapist and how to survive being the parent of an anorectic. As I have already said there are good resources available on-line but I also have a desire to set something up, so go to www. abcofeatindisorders.com and sign up for advance information. Specific things will be offered for these three groups.

If you are a sufferer of anorexia I do hope you feel that I have caught something of your experience in these pages, and, if I have, do please let me know by writing an on-line review wherever you bought this book from. Thank you.

If you are a parent or wife or husband or friend of someone who has anorexia I hope this book has given you a realistic idea of how challenging recovery can be, but has also given you the belief that it can happen.

For an anorectic the key to opening the door is often an unexpected one. Camilla Batmangelli, founder of Kid's Company in the UK, which offers an innovative and multi-faceted programme for children who live on the streets says that surprise does it. Surprise is a powerful intervention. One woman I know stopped being anorectic when she saw a photograph of herself sunbathing. She was lying down and wearing a large hat which shaded her face. She didn't know it was her. She said, 'That woman is too thin'. I said, 'It's you, Karen' and that anorectic door simply opened. Colwyn Travarthen's research with newborns found the same thing. Surprise is a great way to learn.

I am aware that I have not written in detail about how to get someone to sit down and eat, and what to feed them. There are many other much better-informed and more experienced practitioners that do that. My own focus is trying to shift the heart and the mind so that appetite goes from being forbidden to being allowed.

Anorexia has the highest mortality rate of any psychiatric disease. It is an up-front-in-your-face problem. It is unmistakable. Bulimia is something else. Many anorectics, Hubert Lacey, Professor of Psychiatry who is the Director of the Eating Disorder Service at St. Georges Hospital, suggests 60% of anorectics have bulimic symptoms. Others think it is much lower, around 20 to 30%. The next book in the series is *B is for Bulimia: Bulimia Nervosa Explained*. The format will be similar to this book and will explore the land of the bulimic. Many recovering anorectics visit bulimia on their way to getting better. For many anorectics bulimia is their worst nightmare. But it is, as anorexia is, an attempted solution to the problem of how to be in the world. Bulimics who are normal weight or above don't have the intense addiction to hunger itself. Although in terms of years bulimia often lasts longer than anorexia, in my experience bulimics are more attached to life and hope, and so are easier to reach and help. I hope you will want to join me in trying to make sense of that most secretive of eating disorders, bulimia.

Thank you so much for buying and reading this book. If you have enjoyed it, please do leave a review at whatever website you purchased it from.

About the Author

Em Farrell first trained as a counsellor when she was a university student. Her main teacher in massage work was Barry Pluke and her first psychotherapy training was with Antioch University, at Regent's College School of Psychotherapy and Counselling. She has worked with eating disordered patients since she set up a Centre for Eating Disorders in 1989. She worked with over 200 bulimic and anorectic patients using CBT and massage therapy to help them. She then broadened her practice but retained her interest in eating problems. Her book *Lost for Words: the Psychoanalysis of Anorexia and Bulimia* was published in 1995. She worked for several years as the on-line columnist for eating disorders and body image problems for Psychologies Magazine. She ran short courses on Eating Disorders for psychotherapists and counsellors across London and the UK including offering a certificate course in Eating Disorders at the Westminster Pastoral Foundation. She finished a further training in Intensive Short Term Dynamic Psychotherapy in 2012. She is now writing *B is for Bulimia: Bulimia Nervosa Explained*. She lives and works in London but spends a fair amount of time in a field with her horse in Buckinghamshire, where she practices as an equine assisted psychotherapist.

She has developed a bespoke non-residential anorectic treatment programme for sufferers and their families or whoever is involved in their care. You can find more information about this at www.abcofeatingdisorders.com.

Acknowledgements

I can never express my gratitude enough to those women who have shared their stories, their bodies and their hearts with me. My hope is this book captures something of the horror and the hope that is found when someone is anorectic. My thanks also goes to Vic Johnson whose eBook programme finally kick started me on this project that has been brewing inside me since I finished by first book, which is 20 years ago now. I would like to thank my intensive short term psychotherapy teachers Allan Abbass, Josette ten Have-de Labije and most particularly my main teacher Robert Neborsky. The model they work with has helped me become a much better therapist than I was. My daughter Jess, always inspires me and has helped me keep going with this project when my own super-ego gave me a difficult time with it. Lastly a big thank you to Gillian Hinshelwood for lending me her beautiful horse Flare who continues to teach me how to become more grounded, focused, compassionate and contented regardless of the challenges that the environment throws at us.

A big thank you goes to Janet Treasure, Gráinne Smith, Anna Crane, Hilde Bruch, Geraldine Shipton, Marilyn Lawrence, Gianna Williams, Kim Chernin, Kathryn Zerbe, Todd Tucker and Harold Boris. Without their work this book would not have been possible.

Thank you Bob Young, Zozi Goodman and Chastity of Determinedforus on Fiverr.com for editing and proof reading this book. It is a much better read as a result of your hard work. Thank you.

Lastly, a thank you to Bojan of PixelStudio on Fiverr who helped create the covers of all the books in the series.

Other Books by Em Farrell

This book *A is for Anorexia: Anorexia Nervosa Explained* is the first in the series of 'An ABC of Eating Disorders'. The next is *B is for Bulimia: Bulimia Nervosa Explained* and the third will be *C is for Compulsive Eating: Binge Eating and Obesity Explained*.

Her first book *Lost for Words: The Psychoanalysis of Anorexia and Bulimia* is available as an ebook at Amazon.

Offers

Find at www.abcofeatingdisorders.com

For everyone: a FREE Audio Book

A is for Anorexia: Anorexia Nervosa Explained (Route One)

* * *

For parents, family and friends

A FREE monthly support webinar with Em Farrell

* * *

For psychotherapists and counsellors a free chapter 'Body Products and Transitional Phenomena' from *Lost for Words: The Psychoanalysis of Anorexia and Bulimia* by Em Farrell

These are available at www.abcofeatingdisorders.com

Lightning Source UK Ltd.
Milton Keynes UK
UKOW04f1648270917
309982UK00002B/473/P